Tales of Torfaen

W.G. Lloyd

ISBN 0 9520543 5 3

Printed by Hackman Print
Cambrian Industrial Estate, Clydach Vale, Tonypandy
(01443) 441100

CONTENTS

FOREWORD

This book of short stories relating mainly to the Torfaen Valley is produced to comply with the many requests of people who enjoy the subject of local history.

Very often the truth is so much more amazing than fiction and the following pages contain no less than pure local history obtained during many years of research.

If this small volume helps to motivate any clear-minded young local history writers to give the long hours of research necessary to produce an original manuscript of quality, then I will be well pleased.

W.G. Lloyd, July 2000.

ACKNOWLEDGEMENTS

I wish to thank the following for their kindness and positive help during the lengthy research period which made this narrative possible:

Joyce Brown
Neil Carey
Derek Dance
Margaret Dunstan
Bill Davies
Emily Donoghue
Lily Farr
Arthur I. Griffiths
Ethel Hughes
Andrea Jones
Glyn Jones
Elvet Jones
Maurice Jones
Grace Lewis
Jennie Meredith
Richard T. Moore
Bernard Moreton
Eric Parfitt
Aubrey Poole
Bill Powell
Keith Stone
Marjorie Stone
Phyllis Watters
Vera Williams

THE LOST TREASURE of
LLANTARNAM CHURCH

t. Michael of All Angels Church, Llantarnam, is one of the most beautiful churches' in the Eastern Valley of Gwent. An appropriated church of Llantarnam Abbey, there is a strong suggestion that the site held a Celtic cell or retreat before the early church was built and long before the ancient abbey came into existence. During Norman times the early church was altered or replaced by a more substantial building whose walls were extremely thick and, if necessary, would have provided defence instead of a place of worship.

Alterations in the 13th century proved necessary whilst records show that further sweeping changes took place when the building became monastic property in the 15th century.

By 1859 the ancient church presented a comfortless and neglected appearance. Traces of decay had become visible on its damp walls and the pews were heavy and old fashioned causing considerable discomfort to the congregation. This unhappy state of affairs brought about a parish meeting which resulted in the formation of a committee to supervise the much needed work of restoration. These gentlemen met with a ready response and with over £200 in hand the work began.

In no time the unsightly gallery over the western entrance had been moved and the choir was to occupy a place in the chancel. The new pews were of deal and provided comfortable open sittings. The clear staining effect of the arched roof of the nave and chancel corresponded with that of the pews and gave a light and pleasing appearance. A decision to put a new window in the

chancel caused brief excitement when during the progression of work a fine stone arch separating the nave from the chancel, and covered with whitewash, was exposed to view. With a new lighting arrangement enhancing the desirable work undertaken, re-opening services took place at the ancient church in September 1869.

The following year would see extensive work carried out to the Blewitt Chapel which adjoins the parish church. A partition of lath and plaster, with cumbersome worm eaten doors, divided the chapel from the church. These were taken down and two fine stone archways, of ancient date, were left to form an entrance. Around the chapel walls were found not only memorials to the Blewitt family, but also to the former influential families of Kemys and Blount. Other ancient memorials were found, but due to age and decay were not decipherable, although one gave the date 1591.

More ancient secrets of the parish church came to light in 1921 when further restoration work revealed wonderful things.

By 1921 the rural spot of Llantarnam had become quite a popular outer suburb. The church of St. Michael could be found standing back from the main road in what was then regarded as a large graveyard. A row of tall elm trees formed a welcome shade from the fierce heat of the afternoon summer sun as workmen commenced further restoration work. A Newport builder by the name of William Davies received the contract for the work due to considerable experience in church restoration and he had recently carried out excellent work on St. Woollos Cathedral, Newport.

It was to some extent fortunate that this careful man was vigilant when he scraped away some of the old plaster covering the interior of the nave walls. Many coatings of lime and colour wash were removed before an extraordinary discovery became visible. What began to take place before his astonished eyes was a number of mural paintings on the old facing of the nave walls and in their original medieval colourings of dark red and brown paint.

When hearing of the discovery Mr. Kyrle Fletcher, a Monmouthshire historian and a representative of the South Wales Argus, visited the church. Upon arrival, the vicar at once took him along to the nave of the church and showed the wall on the left hand side where a portion of the stone work had been cleaned. Fletcher found that the wall had only been cleaned down in places but enough was revealed to give an excellent impression of the early wall decoration which consisted of figures painted in a dark red brown paint and in curious long strokes. The largest part uncovered prior to his visit showed the figure, presumed by him to be a lady, in wide flowing robes and wearing a beaver hat, not unlike the popular Welsh hat once worn by the women of Wales.

Further along, on the same wall, a smaller figure had been uncovered, which looked like a priest in robes. He observed that the crude wall drawings strongly resembled the figures previously uncovered on the walls of the church at Llantwit Major, in the Vale of Glamorgan.

Realising the importance of the discovery of the old work the vicar called in Archbishop Green and the well known architect Harold Breakspear who had worked on Windsor Castle. Under their supervision the whole of the old work in the nave was uncovered revealing a magnificent set of medieval wall paintings probably executed by the Cistercian monks from the nearby abbey.

The north wall revealed a picture of Our Lady enthroned with a boy server in robes in attendance and a priest in medieval costume. The south wall revealed paintings of saints, John the Baptist and Elija in the Wilderness, while over the chancel arch were large figures of floating angels. This was thought by some to be the great picture of Doom which was generally placed in the parish church and showed the resurrection of the dead, with the last judgement, and angels carrying off souls into heaven and demons dragging others into hell.

This was the bible of the people of the parish who could not read and was for ever before their eyes as an eternal lesson.

It was probably during the Reformation that all this work at Llantarnam was covered up with whitewash and large texts placed there instead.

Unfortunately for the discovered paintings, after exposure to air they gradually deteriorated and within several weeks they had crumbled away and no drawings or photographs remain to give an impression of what the Llantarnam nave really looked like.

In 1939, included in several further important architectural finds, a substantial line of solid quoin stones (corner stones) was uncovered behind the organ and in the west wall of the Lady Chapel.

Who knows what other secrets remain at the site of this venerable old church.

JOHN JERIMIAH-MORGAN

 he road became steeper and my breathing more laboured while progressing further up into the high country. Each enquiry to the whereabouts of Holly Tree Cottage, Garndiffaith, met with little response until a clear-minded young gentleman replied, "Just ask where the ducks are." Sure enough, within minutes, I stood before a magnificent duck pond, (which would thrill any young accompanied child) and also a delightful cottage where John Jerimiah-Morgan, a 94 year old Waterloo veteran, expired in 1887.

The trek had been well worth it when I thought of the elderly veteran moving slowly to the bedroom window to see the local part-time, red-coated Volunteers pass his cottage while on a training march.

Born John Jerimiah around 1792, in Goytre, a parish which seems to consist of either Morgan or Jerimiah families at that time, he would later add Morgan to his surname. Employment as an agricultural worker held very little appeal when the 19th century was young, and the Goytre lad first enlisted in the Monmouthshire Militia before joining the renowned Royal Welch Fusiliers.

Time spent with Wellington in the Peninsula campaigns took its toll on the young man, but he would live to take part in one of the most talked about battles of any war.

John Jerimiah-Morgan

It is amazing to realise that when the battle of Waterloo depended on the outcome of the thunderous charges of the French cuirassiers, led by Marshal Ney, on the British squares, John Jerimiah-Morgan, of Garndiffaith, was in the thick of it.

He, with three cousins and Isaac James, of Trevethin, nearby, stood his ground in the squares amid the smoke of shell and musket fire. Men fell around him as the brave 23rd held on and Napoleon lost the battle of Waterloo.

Private Morgan spent some time seeing the sights in Paris with the army of occupation before eventually being discharged in Limerick, Ireland. It was here he met Catherine, an Irish girl, and they married in both Protestant and Roman Catholic Churches.

Much of his working life on his return to the Eastern Valley was spent in agriculture and as a stone quarryman.

When he died hundreds of people lined the roads on either side from Coomb's Cross to St. Thomas's Church, Talywain, and witnessed the passage of the Union Jack draped coffin which held the highly esteemed Waterloo veteran. John West, of Pontypool, another Waterloo veteran, who would live to 100 years, shed a tear as his friend was laid to rest.

The sad event was mostly forgotten until 1915, when, on the hundredth anniversary of the battle of Waterloo, an appeal went out to correctly mark the grave and replace a small headstone protruding barely eighteen inches out of the ground. Probably due to hardships during the Great War, the appeal fell on deaf ears and the veteran's grandson, Mr James Carey, of Viaduct Road, Garndiffaith, had little chance to supply further details to any interested parties.

Descending the valley road with the evening light quickly turning to shadows, I thought a last glance over the churchyard wall would be a mark of respect for a local man who took part in one of the most wondrous chapters in world history. Under a tree in the corner of the redundant graveyard I'm sure I momentarily saw an old soldier standing while resting on his musket. The moonlight seemed to glint on something at the front of his tall Shako helmet and this could only have been the proud badge of the Royal Welch Fusiliers.

A FLYER IN PONTYPOOL

lying Officer D.R.S. Bader (pronounced Bahder) had made the Combined Services rugby team and it was expected that his selection would make him the natural choice to play at fly-half for England. His recent form for the Royal Air Force rugby team had been exceptional. Frequently, the headlines on the sport's page of the Times read "Bader Brilliant" or "Bader Excels," and regularly he would be mentioned as the most accomplished player on the field. During his schooldays he had shone at sport, particularly rugger, and whether in games or day-to-day events he always had the positive habit of cutting through irrelevancies to get to the heart of the matter.

In March, 1931, the rugby minded population of Pontypool would have the unique opportunity to see the dazzling skills of the short, strongly built man, who was to become a legend.

The Royal Air Force rugby team arrived in Pontypool for the first time. Their fullback, unable to find the valley town, did not turn up and subsequently Sam Williams, of Pontypool, substituted for the visitors. Although the Pontypool team were soundly beaten, the regular, enthusiastic crowd at the Recreation Ground would witness the season's most spectacular game.

Bader was at his best. His touch kicking broke the hearts of the Pontypool forwards and with two outstanding centres at his elbow, he caused havoc with the defence. Even in those days the Pontypool supporters quickly recognised a man before his time and their applause was fair and vociferous.

The Royal Air Force rugby team won the game by 22 points to 9 points. On one occasion Bader completely beat Gwyn Bayliss, the Pontypool full-back by strong running and a swerve at the precise moment to score a good try.

Douglas Bader

14

Flying Officer Douglas Bader would not play rugby for England or return the following season to Pontypool. Already possessing a natural ability to fly aeroplanes the young man was a member of the R.A.F. aerobatics team and had found an equal to his sporting interests. As with all individuals who shine, a mischievous remark, which intended to slap the young man down, caused him to demonstrate a low flying technique that was to end in tragedy.

In front of a small group of fellow pilots Bader gave a rare personal display of his tremendous flying ability. With the flight almost over and only the low flying stunt to complete, disaster struck. With the Bulldog aeroplane glinting in the sun, Bader was fast rolling out of a complicated manoeuvre when the left wing-tip touched the ground. As the propeller and cowling dug into the earth causing a shower of debris, the displaced engine could be seen bouncing along in a cloud of dust. The aeroplane continued to cartwheel until coming to rest in a crumbled mass. As the dust began to settle the men by the clubhouse were seen to be running towards the wreckage.

While regaining consciousness and aware of the blood spurting from a leg wound, his first thought was: "Damn! I won't be able to play rugger on Saturday."

He would never play rugby again. With the amputation of both legs the young man would later find well-deserved recognition in a more serious arena. His determination to be the first to use artificial legs without the use of any support inspired countless other disabled people. A return to flying in those days would only be described as remarkable. With the outbreak of World War II, the former Harlequins fly-half would be one of the few who took part in the aerial Battle of Britain. Although senior Royal Airforce personnel shunted the disabled Bader into a post commanding a back up squadron, he would have none of it and was soon in the thick of the action. At a time when a pilot was considered to be an 'ace' after shooting down five enemy aircraft, Bader's final count was over twenty.

His luck in the air eventually ran out and after being shot down and captured by the Germans, he was sent to the infamous Kolditz prison for prisoners-of-war who were determined to escape.

It would be ten years after the exceptional display of rugby skill at Pontypool when a local newspaper reminded the connoisseurs of the handling game who the famous pilot was; and some still appreciate the privilege of seeing, on a cold winter day, the man who would a second time, reach for the sky under extraordinary circumstances.

As the years rolled by Douglas Bader left an example to mankind which became a legend. All agreed when his autobiography concluded with the words, 'Some hand not of this world may be using Bader as a vessel bearing another lesson for Man in his struggle.'

THE BATTLE AT RED RIVER

ccompanied by a cloud of dust, the 4th US Cavalry moved out of Fort Concho with orders to find and detain the hostile Cheyenne Indians who carried on a lucrative trade in stolen livestock and the exchange of hostages along the West Texas frontier.

Unknown to Irish born Mr and Mrs Mahoney, of West Street, Pontypool, their son was about to become the only Welshman to win the American equivalent of our Victoria Cross.

Born in Pontypool on May 2nd, 1850, Gregory Patrick Mahoney grew up in the ancient town only to find employment unavailable by the time he had reached maturity.

The land of opportunity beckoned the blue-eyed young man with blonde hair and it is believed that he arrived in America in mid-1871.

Unable to find employment as a labourer in Boston, Massachusetts, he enlisted in the US Cavalry on November 8th, 1871.

As a member of an elite scouting detachment, the Pontypool man earned extra pay for the extremely hazardous duty, but it was as a member of Company E leaving Fort Concho that he achieved distinction.

While searching the headwaters of the Red River for the main Indian encampment, the first battalion went into camp at Tule Canyon on the evening of the 26th, September, 1874. When realising that the blue-coated soldiers were intent on destroying their camp, the Indians tried diversionary tactics to lead the column in another direction and planned to steal their horses. This would place the troopers in an extremely vulnerable position and at the mercy of the rugged terrain.

The following night, Private Mahoney drew horse guard duty with around ten other troopers. Their duty was to control the command's horses in the event of various contingencies. Among these might be stampedes caused by attacking Indians, buffaloes intermingling, the presence of snakes and lightening strikes.

The Indians went after the horses early in the morning. Mahoney, along with Corporal of the Guard, Edwin Phoenix, were the first two men to mount their horses and charge into the attacking Cheyenne, estimated to be around thirty in number. Mahoney and Phoenix emptied their Colt .45 pistols at the expense of many redskin's lives. They continued in amongst the Cheyenne and using their pistols as clubs, fought hand-to-hand with the Cheyenne warriors.

Upon sight of the approaching remainder of the guard and supporting troops, the Cheyenne broke off and fled to the Southwest.

The tremendous courage of the two men no doubt saved the expedition from disaster. At the time of the incident the temperature had climbed as high as 110 degrees and an acute shortage of water was an immediate concern. Also, a lack of grass for the horses, after a plague of locusts had cleared the region, added to the growing list of problems.

The main Indian camp was found shortly afterwards with dire repercussions to its occupants.

For his brave action, Private Mahoney, Company E, 4th United States Cavalry, received the Medal of Honor while stationed at Fort Elliot, Texas, on January 28th, 1876. There is no evidence of a formal award ceremony. He probably received the medal like so many other Indian Wars recipients when it was delivered by registered mail via stagecoach.

What happened to Gregory Patrick Mahoney after he was discharged on

Medal of Honor

November 8th, 1876, remains a mystery. Extensive searches in America did not find him. His parents died within a week of each other in West Street, Pontypool, during August 1897, and nothing indicates that Greg Mahoney was in the Pontypool district up to that time.

The Medal of Honor Historical Society are keen to know of his post-army career.

THE CEDAR of LEBANON

he following report concerning the recently built Monmouthshire Canal, written in 1802, gave industrial entrepreneurs an insight into the benefits this improved method of transport could bring to an area rich in natural resources:

"The bowels of the earth here are loaded with minerals - hitherto unsought for and little known - merely for the want of such a conveyance to market. This now obtained, old mines will be explored, new ones discovered, and Mother Earth ransacked for her treasures. Nor will the forests on her surface longer remain neglected; all will yield to the converted hand of industry. Possessions will be greatly increased in value and the labourer will find lasting food for his perseverance with ores of iron and lead, stone and lime quarries, timber trees etc., which by so ready a conveyance to the Bristol Channel will spread not only over England but the world."

This new and profitable situation undoubtedly brought George Conway and his family to the Cwmbran area.

Sir Joseph Alfred Bradney, in his splendid 'History of Monmouthshire', states that George Conway came to Monmouthshire from Melin-Griffith, in Glamorgan. It is known that he arrived in Caerleon prior to 1770 with his wife and father-in-law John Jenkins, who managed the local iron works. George assisted his father-in-law in managing the ironworks and documentary evidence shows that the young man was baptised in the Baptist Church at Caerleon in 1775.

By 1800, Cwmbran was little more than a sparsely populated district consisting of a few scattered hamlets in which the menfolk were mainly concerned with agricultural needs.

This pastoral setting was to change when George Conway left the Caerleon works in 1802 to construct his own iron and tinplate works on the banks of the Avon Llywd at Pontnewydd. By this time he and his three sons had become acknowledged experts in the trade and his eldest son would, in 1806, start a second tinplate works at Pontrhydyrun (The bridge of the ford of the ash trees). This became the Edlogan Works at the bottom of Chapel Lane, Pontrhydyrun.

George Conway and his family settled in Pontrhydyrun and lived near their heavy industrial undertakings. Throughout his life George Conway had believed in the Baptist cause and with his works giving employment in the area, which in turn greatly increased the local population, he not only realised the religious needs of the district, but was in a financial position to help.

The first intimation of this caring attitude was when the younger members of the Conway family commenced a Sunday School for the local children in 1807. Held in the Assorting Room of the Edlogan Works, the project proved a success with a full service occasionally held and Reverend Micah Thomas, of Abergavenny, attending.

However, the popularity of the enterprise would suffer a set back when the conditions under which the classes were held became unhealthy and other options had to be considered.

A more substantial place of worship would become a priority and inspired William, George Conway's eldest son, to donate a parcel of land at the top of the Pontrhydyrun hill. Here, the foundation of a new chapel was laid on the 13th May, 1815, and at the cost of £600, the improved place of worship opened on the 15th, November of the same year.

The first members of the new independent Baptist Chapel were George Conway, his wife, three sons and three daughters. These were soon joined by Mr. John Charles, who was made the first deacon, and Mrs Cridland.

The historical religious and legal papers relating to this period, and later times, is still to be found in the archives of the church.

The first Pontrhydyrun Baptist Church served the followers well but by 1836 the congregation grew to around 100 members and again improvements became necessary. The building of the present day impressive edifice commenced in 1836 though not opened for worship until August 16th, 1837. The cost was £2000 and it opened free of any debt.

At this time the burial ground was also enlarged due to acquired land and a most interesting fact of the church history then took place.

Near the new entrance to the church and in two other corners of the burial ground, seedlings were buried with loving hands. Believed to have been brought home by a member of the Conway family who had been on a pilgrimage to the Holy Land, the seedlings thrived splendidly through the fleeting intervening years and the Cedars of Lebanon became renowned throughout the district.

The Cedrus Libani did not grow in any great numbers in Israel in ancient times, but grew in great forests on the western slopes of the Lebanon mountains. This is why the kings David and Solomon had to negotiate with Hiram of Tyre for timber to build their palaces and Temple (2 Chronicle 2:3, 8).

In 1906, the largest ever known meeting, up to that time, of the Monmouthshire English Baptists was held at the Pontryhydyrun Church and many of the delegates would remark enthusiastically of the cedar tree by the gate, which they had just passed through. Thought by many to be the finest they had seen, it possessed a diameter of some five feet and spread its fine umbrageous branches over a wide space on all sides.

The three cedars of Lebanon planted almost one hundred years previously, continued to enhance the magnificent work carried out by the well-attended church until 1928.

In November of that year what can only be described as a hurricane, and the worst in living memory, caused tremendous damage throughout the county. With many buildings losing their roofs and hundreds of trees up-rooted, the Pontryhydyrun Baptist Church was not to escape the devastation.

Sadly, two of the cedar trees were hurled to the ground leaving only the one near the main gate still standing.

Throughout the centuries the Pontrhydyrun Baptist Church continued to prosper due to the devotion and hard work of its members. As one passes this now ancient and stately edifice, pause for a moment and look at the remaining cedar of Lebanon, standing as a lone sentinel guarding the way to the House of the Lord, and witness to the Christian love of generations of Cwmbran folk.

LOCAL HERO'S NAME STILL LIVES ON

s Avril Williams, from Lincoln, had little knowledge of events during the great slaughter of World War One until occupying an old farm-house in Auchonvilliers, France.

Her ambition of turning the farm-house into a successful guest house and tea-rooms would soon be realised and the time when murderous artillery shells screamed over the ancient homestead had long passed.

It was not until work commenced in the old cellar beneath the upgraded building that a remarkable discovery came to light. Etched in the walls of this former dark room could be seen the names and regiments of soldiers who had taken advantage of what little shelter was available from the shelling during those difficult times.

Possibly used as a first-aid post, the walls of the cellar revealed the names of brave men who are no longer with us and one name which stands out clearer than most others is that of:

Pte. H. Weaver 3076,
Coy Stretcher Bearer,
2nd Mons Regt.

Varteg born Henry (Harry) Weaver lived in the home of his young wife at 6 Hill Street, Pontnewynydd and he joined up at the beginning of the long war before going out to the front on March 17th, 1915. He and George Weaver survived the carnage while another member of the family, William Butcher, lies buried in a foreign land.

Harry came home and was employed for most of his life as a collier in Varteg Slope Colliery. His only son Tom moved away taking with him Harry's two grandsons, Hugh and Terry. With the passage of time, Harry became a champion pigeon breeder and belonged to the still popular Garndiffaith Pigeon Club. He raced the South Road and returned to France to win the famous national open race of Bordeaux, and also those of Thurso and Perth.

Alice Weaver died at an early age and it would be some time later, in February 1959, the esteemed veteran passed away, in his lodgings, Neath Villas, Varteg, at the age of 64 years.

Military enthusiasts are at the present time visiting the area to record and trace the owners of the names engraved in the stone and a good quality photograph of Pte. Henry Weaver, in uniform, now takes pride of place on the wall of the dinning room in the pleasant guest house in Auchonvilliers.

THE MAN IN BLACK

omeone suggested that there must be 15,000 spectators at least in the packed grandstand and completely covering the grass slope on the opposite side of the competition ring. Not a blade of grass was left uncovered on the incline which allowed a splendid view of the events taking place to mark the Monday Whitson Bank Holiday in 1947. Crowds had flocked to Pontypool Park from not only Monmouthshire, but also the surrounding counties, and in brilliant sunshine, it proved to be a colourful spectacle as the people of all ages ate their sandwiches and drank tea from flasks while they waited for the main event to take place. It was promised to be an afternoon unique in the annals of the Eastern Valley of Monmouthshire, and, as the Regimental Band of the South Wales Borderers marched up and down while playing its stirring music, the mood of the large crowd was reaching fever pitch. The time was at last near for those who had only seen the main attraction in Pathe News reports at local cinemas.

The small man arrived at the Pontypool Park gates to an enormous reception and was reverently escorted to the holiday fete while besieged by autograph hunters en-route. A few minutes was spent changing into his famous black running suit before an announcement was made and the visitor received a tremendous welcome from the huge crowd. Sidney Wooderson was already a legend. He held four world records for middle distance running and in all probability an Olympic medal would have come his way but for a cracked bone in his ankle prior to the games. Only through the good fortune of having a close friend of the famous athlete working in the Pontypool district did the local people have the opportunity to see the world record holder while he was still at his peak.

In his black running suit the thin, bespectacled man, who weighed less than nine stone, did a warm up half mile and signed autographs while waiting for his race to commence.

In athletic conditions very different to those of today Wooderson was a man born before his time. Not only did he win important events, but he also entertained with an electrifying sprint at the end of a race. Born in August 1914, just after the outbreak of the Great War, the conditions which prevailed during the first ten years of his life were not those which would help a future world record holder. As a schoolboy he ran the fastest mile for his age group and from there he never looked back. Soon after he would beat the famous Jack Lovelock and later Lauri Pihka the Finnish expert said: "The English knew what they were talking about when they asked us to wait until we had seen Wooderson. His style is indescribably easy - he runs like an unharnessed horse, as though he runs for the sheer joy of the movement." In fact one of the main features of Wooderson's running was that he would be so perfectly balanced that even when severely bustled he always managed to get back into his stride with the minimum of effort and lost time. His rather upright body carriage and high swinging-across-the-body arm action seemed to trouble the purist who maintained that Wooderson was "no stylist" but his action had an eloquence of smoothness, power and relaxation. Many of his races would be won in a dramatic sprint for the finishing tape. At the age of 32 years he won a 5000m race by 30m to record the second fastest time ever, and in the race was the future, great Olympic champion, Emile Zatopek. Employment as a solicitor's clerk in London kept him busy during the day and consequently his all-weather training had to be done in evenings following business hours. His sober life style in all probability helped him to recover in 1944 from a serious rheumatic illness which everyone thought would end his track career.

The starting gun echoed around the Pontypool Park and immediately it became not a race but the rare occasion in the lives of local people when they forgot their humdrum existence and were transfixed with the sight of a small man appearing to almost float around four laps of the track. As the man in black effortlessly stretched his legs the remaining competitors were only humans as this creature sent by the gods took up the lead and was out on his own. Time seemed to stand still as the ghost-like figure circled the track and it was only when he breasted the tape that the magical spell was broken. Some 20m behind came Austen Littler, the record breaker's friend and a creditable third on that memorable afternoon was the red-vested, veteran, Welsh cross country champion and International, Harry Gallivan, of Sebastopol.

Sydney Wooderson

The local people who were privileged to witness this rare event in Pontypool Park all those years ago first thought no man looked less like the popular image of a world champion athlete than the small man with round spectacles. He was not even possessed by good health. Yet this was a man who won his way into the hearts of a nation with his world records and courageous running. As he moved into his stride he would leave no doubt in the minds of people who watched in awe that he was the benefactor of a remarkable gift.

WHICH ONE WILL THE FOUNTAIN BLESS?

I s the age of romance dead in the Eastern Valley? What has happened to the passion for a way of life which our ancestors expressed with so much success and subsequently brought a warmth into the lives of past generations?

Even the old Squire took his wife on honeymoon to Italy! The extensive travels in the warm climate enchanted Mrs Hanbury so much that a considerable number of exotic trees and plants were brought home to Pontypool Park to form what we now know as the Italian Gardens. The birth of a son and heir to the ageing Squire was later commemorated by the building of the nearby Italian styled Pontypool Town Hall.

During the early part of the 20th century Mr Roderick's popular Town Band could be regularly heard enthusiastically playing in the Italian Garden, but this now is only a distant memory.

In 1959, the gardens again became a popular place to visit when the old lily pond, so overgrown with weeds, was replaced by a new centrepiece.

A fountain in the form of a hollow, concrete dragon, produced by Walter Brown, a member of the Council's staff, proved an excellent idea especially when painted with a lead-based red paint.

Four jets of water appeared from the dragon's mouth and reached a height of about twenty metres. For a short

time this display was further enhanced in the evenings by a revolving tri-coloured disc which gave the effect of the water being red, green and blue.

Was it a coincidence that the new fountain followed not long after the release of the popular film *Three Coins In A Fountain* and the recording of the hit song; both based on the legend of the fountain of Trevi, in Rome? Romantically minded inhabitants of the Pontypool district were not slow in throwing a silver coin over their shoulder and into the fountain while making a silent wish.

The fountain is no more!

Fountain of Trevi, Rome

With the Italian Garden again being improved around ten years ago a sledgehammer was accidentally introduced to the concrete dragon and yet another valley treasure became lost for all time. What remains of the pond seems to have developed into a container for beer cans and other rubbish.

Perhaps as a sign of hope for the future a gathering of young people, who, without the motives of high-profiling or self-elevation, will form a 'Friends of the Valley' and work with the necessary departments to improve our natural assets? Due to the topography of the land are we not in a unique position to have the most beautiful valley in Britain?

Will the fountain of Pontypool come to life again, and if so, who will the fountain bless?

LLANDERFEL

et another treasure of the Torfaen Valley lies out of sight and almost forgotten at this time when at last an awareness of the fragility of our local history is slowly surfacing in the minds of those who should take responsibility for our ancient past. The former monument in question, on the slopes of the Mynydd Maen (Mountain of Stone) near Upper Cwmbran, is thought to date from about 550 AD., thus being, probably, the oldest building in the valley.

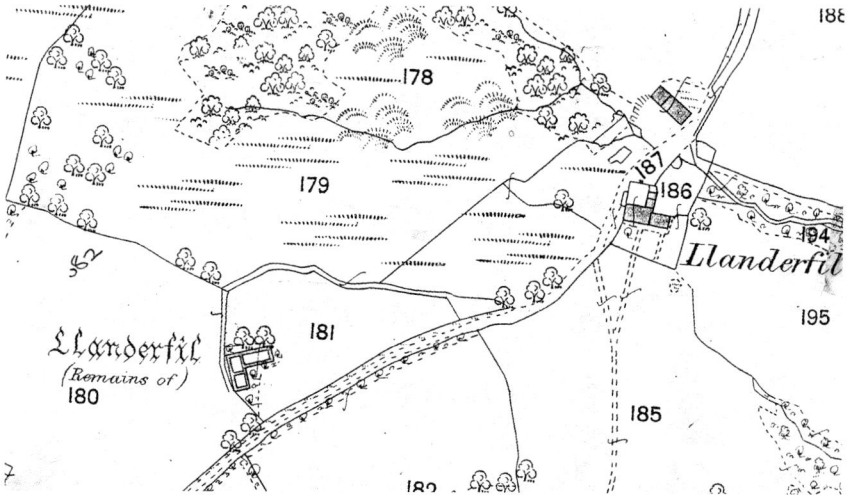

Ordinance Survey Map, 1880

Between 1904 and 1933, Sir Joseph Bradney wrote in his extensive History of Monmouthshire the following:

> *This ancient church, of which only the ruins are left, stands in the upper part of the parish (Llantarnam) on the side of the Mynydd Maen at an elevation of nearly 1000 feet above sea level.*
>
> *Derfel Gadarn (Derval the Strong) a celebrated warrior in the time of King Arthur, distinguished himself at the battle of Camlan in 542. The latter part of his life was devoted to religion, and he founded this church and Llandderfel in Merionethshire. At the latter are preserved what are considered relics of Derfel, part of a wooden horse and wooden crosier, called Ceffyl Derfel and Ffon Dervel. There was also in that church a*

28

wooden image said to be of Derfel which was taken to London and burnt at Smithfield in May 1538.

Nothing seems to be known as to when this church came to be disused and allowed to get into disrepair. The ruins of the walls are no more than two or three feet high, out of which at the east end are growing beech trees of considerable age, giving the appearance of it having been a ruin for 200 years.

The shape of the building is remarkable, for it comprises of two wings at right angles, which appear to have been divided by a wall.

Llanderfel in later times was part of the possessions of the monks of Llantarnam, and so came to the Morgans of that place.

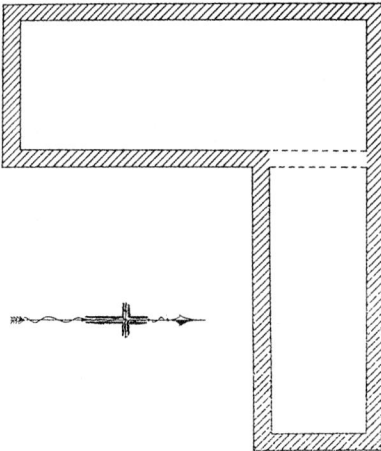

PLAN OF RUINED CHURCH AT LLANDDERFEL.
Scale: $\frac{1}{18}$ inch = 1 foot.

The unusual plan of two small buildings at right angles to each, probably comprised of a small nave with eastern choir and a small south chapel.

Throughout the following centuries the land containing this ancient Monmouthshire shrine would come into the possession of various owners, but it is known to have been still in use in 1535 when the Valor Ecclesiasticus recorded Capella S'ti Dervalli' as bringing 26s. 8d. to the Llantarnam Abbey in oblations.

The chapel was built directly over a seam of coal which outcrops very near the surface, in fact scratching about with a pick will reveal the mineral. During the great strike of 1926 this area was the scene of much activity when local people dug small pits for coal.

During World War Two, the policy of German aircraft to discard any unused bombs in order to lighten their load before crossing the Channel, and not to return to base with weapons which should have landed on a target, caused them to drop their implements of death in the Torfaen Valley. Several of these landed about a hundred metres from the site of the chapel and killed a few cows belonging to the nearby Llanderfel Farm. The next day, a Sunday, hundreds of people from the Cwmbran village walked up the Mynydd Maen to inspect this spot while at the same time trampling down crops and young trees in their excitement. Many of them must have walked over the venerable ruins of the old chapel and not realised they were there.

In the mid-twentieth century there was a small attempt at excavating the site by amateur archaeologists, but with the memories still clear of the local invasion of his land during the recent world war, the work was understandably stopped by the farmer. Perhaps in the not too distant future a professional excavation may take place at the site and the decision of the farmer all those years ago will no doubt be regarded as an act of Providence. At that time very few of the old stone were left. It was thought the stone had been carted off to the surrounding farms and used for building.

For many years the ancient treasure lay in a small wood standing at the foot of the Mynydd Maen and at the bottom of a pathway known as the 'The Slippery Path'. Hardly recognisable now, the visitor to the spot should dwell awhile and picture in the 'minds eye' the Cistercian monks who cleared the land and farmed many parts of our old valley. This remote and lovely wilderness holds yet another fragile link with our medieval history.

REMARKABLE ANCESTORS

he upsurge of interest in the hobby of tracing ancestors continues at a pace throughout the country with many local people finding their roots while persisting with this revealing research.

Although information about long departed relatives will give a greater understanding of present day circumstances, only a few of the many thousands who follow the trail into the past will find an ancestor who has done something remarkable.

William Powell is one of the few. He grew up in Pontnewynydd and was awarded the British Empire Medal for dedicated service to the railway industry.

Bill did a useful job with the Welsh Guards in Italy during the Second World War, but it is not his war service that he readily talks about.

His father, also named William, of the 2nd Battalion, The Welsh Regiment, won the Military Medal for gallantry and devotion to duty in 1916, when the battalion suffered many casualties around High Wood on the Somme. Mr Powell, senior, completed four years in that conflict and later lived at 2, College Terrace, Pontnewynydd. After being a collier at Tirpentwys Colliery, and an athletics coach in his spare time, he died at Pontypool Hospital, in 1945.

The pride in Bill Powell's voice does not end there. His grandfather, on his mother's side, also did military service in World War One. As an older man, Tom Rose also won the Military Medal when he rescued several men buried during an intense bombardment. Always a quiet man, and a Public Works employee for many years, Tom Rose, MM., died at Pontypool, in 1960.

No best selling novel could read better than the story of Bill's great-grandmother, Elizabeth Rose, and all can be substantiated by documentary evidence.

Born Elizabeth Amos in 1833, at Paulton, Somerset, and whilst in service at the squire's house at Colne, she met Henry Rose, a soldier in the Wiltshire Militia. Soon after their marriage, war broke out, and they left for the headquarters of the Wiltshire Regiment, where they signed on for seven years.

Many women wanted to accompany their men to the Crimea. One dressed as a soldier and marched with the men through the dock gates and onto a transport before being discovered. Mrs Rose did not have that problem, and sailed on the strength of the battalion as a cook to the men.

For five years she remained in the Crimea while carrying out both nursing and cooking duties. During this long period she faced the burning summers and severe winters with the fortitude of a soldier's wife. It was in this unfriendly land that three children were born to her, two who died there, and a third passed away later.

Several times Mrs Rose came into contact with Florence Nightingale; on one occasion being visited by the famous lady while in hospital.

Sebastopol, Crimea. 1854

Retiring to civil life, Henry Rose took up employment as a freestone cutter, but sadly died in a quarry accident. There were eleven children of the marriage, one being Tom Rose, MM.

Mrs Rose, who on her third marriage took the name of Phillips, lived for some years on a farm and had been in business in Newport. In 1918 she came to Pontypool and died nine years later with her children around her in Jubilee Terrace, Wainfelin, Pontypool, at 95 years of age.

STICKS and STONES

ong before the present imposing building came into existence, an ancient cottage public house, known as the Old Crown Inn, served the district well. Found opposite the towpath at Sebastopol, the small hostelry had been popular for many years with the bargees working the Pontnewynydd, Brecon and Newport Canal. It was here that the canal workers took their last refreshments before tackling the flights of locks which would take them to the Newport Docks.

Local farmers also frequented the hostelry and tied their horses to the large oak tree outside the inn before spending the remainder of an evening in musical merriment. Enterprising young local lads earned a small income by arriving in front of the inn a few minutes before closing time and making a great show of pretending to calm any tethered horses. This would be rewarded with a penny from their grateful 'puddled' owners when they emerged into the night air.

Always thought of as a place of relaxation after a day of hard work, it appears that everyone enjoyed the hospitality inside the small hostelry until, a report in the old Monmouthshire Merlin newspaper indicated that a visiting member of the popular journal's staff had somehow been upset:

A SINGULAR FUNERAL

The inmates of a certain hostelry situated in that renowned region called Sebastopol, have recently been plunged into great distress by the demise of the member of the household, a favourite monkey. It will scarcely be credited that the remains of the animal were interred in the presence of a numerous body of mourners; when it is remembered that amongst them were observed several striking family likenesses, the near relationship may serve to account for that affection and regard which were manifested at the loss of a departed brother.

The Monmouthshire Merlin,
February 19th, 1859.

THE ONE THAT GOT AWAY

adly, little remain to remind us of a once busy railway industry within the boundaries of the Eastern Valley. As each generation of former railway employees pass away, and more and more knowledge of a former way of life is lost forever in the mist of forgetfulness, how will future young people know of their contribution to a once thriving valley community?

Who will tell of the locomotive that stood in the sheds at Coedygric on a November night in 1871? Few will know of the panic experienced by the fireman as he stood alone on the footplate and witnessed another locomotive approaching at speed. His only course of action was to jump for it and he would live to see the beginning of a remarkable sequence of events. The collision shunted the stationary engine, with its tender first, up the gentle rise which led to the Monmouthshire line at Griffithstown. This was assisted by the valve of the engine by some means being open. From here the unmanned locomotive gained speed on the incline, passing through Pontnewydd and Cwmbran on its way to Newport. The distance traversed to Newport was about ten miles and the speed of locomotive was such that the journey was covered in as many minutes.

The staff at Mill Street Station, Newport, spoke of an approaching fiery gleam on the line and the sound of a mighty rushing wind as the runaway passed by before instantly vanishing into the darkness. Then the danger increased even more. With a strong incline to Dock Street, the velocity of the runaway 'injin' doubled. The railway-line now passed many wharves alongside the river and a great deal of traffic from the town would cross in front of the runaway. Fortunately the event was taking place at night. For reasons of safety, in those days, around fifteen barriers lay across the railway-line to control the passing traffic. No time was at hand to raise these barriers and residents nearby would hear the splintering of wood and grinding of metal as the locomotive's great force demolished all in its path.

The runaway continued until it reached Waterloo Junction, on the edge of Lord Tredegar's estate. Here, Providence took a hand and the engine's tender jumped the rail before the lot ploughed into an embankment.

Not long after, the engine dispatched from Pontypool Road to look for the missing one, arrived.

The cost of the damage met by the Great Western Railway Company totalled £1000, but thankfully no loss of life or injury occurred due to the unusual event.

THE TRUTH WILL OUT

awrence Spendlove was not bothered what people did, providing they did it peacefully. As a representative of law and order, this philosophy accompanied him throughout a long and distinguished career.

He was born in Pembrokeshire and grew up in India, his father having been an Army schoolmaster. His parents brought him back to England at the age of 14 years. In 1901 he joined the 7th Dragoon Guards before serving with them for eight years, which included periods in South Africa and Egypt.

Entering the Monmouthshire Constabulary in 1909, promotion to sergeant soon followed. On four occasions during his career, he was recommended for the King's Medal for bravery. As a brilliant horseman, much of his time was spent introducing a troop of mounted police into the county. However, it was his early experience as one of the constables who participated in the violent 1911 Tredegar riots, which later proved invaluable.

Arriving in Pontypool as Superintendent in 1923, he already sensed the growing unrest in the valley which would culminate in the miners general strike in 1926.

In July, 1926, a small number of men decided to work at the Quarry Level Colliery, to be found a few miles outside Pontypool. When they finished their shift, around one thousand demonstrators, who regarded them as blacklegs, were in position at the colliery entrance.

Superintendent Spendlove and just seventeen police officers had the unenviable task of escorting the workers through the hostile crowd. Halfway into the melee, stones began to rain down on the police and records show that the Superintendent had no other course of action but to order a baton charge. The demonstrators fled in all directions, and the strike leaders were seen to quickly hide under a nearby railway truck.

The following year, Lawrence H. Spendlove, Superintendent of the Pontypool Division of the Monmouthshire Constabulary, had the MBE conferred upon him for his courage and efficiency on that black day in Eastern Valley history.

On a fine April day in 1929, Superintendent Spendlove married at Risca, the wedding being kept quiet with only a few members of the family present.

In 1950, Lawrence Spendlove, MBE, retired as Deputy Chief Constable of Monmouthshire, to live the remainder of his life contentedly in Skenfrith.

Many senior folk will remember this dedicated officer, sitting astride his well turned out majestic horse, as he led numerous processions along the roads of our valley.

THE KING

he age of steam is now only a memory and no longer do the young lads of the Eastern Valley spend their school summer holidays train spotting along the main railway tracks of the region.

No more will a boy prompt his parents into giving permission, and lunch money, so that he can spend the day at Newport Railway Station with the objective of spotting the 'giants' of the metal road. On the platform of this busy railway station would be found a newsvendor's stall where it was possible to purchase a small book containing the name and number of every locomotive owned by the Great Western Railway. With the arrival of each train, the name of the locomotive would be underlined in the book to record that it had been seen.

During the nineteen-fifties, the lads of the Eastern Valley would not have to go far to see the most famous of all Great Western Railway locomotives. Around 5.30pm each week-day, a King-class engine would arrive at Pontypool Road Station to pick up passengers before continuing towards Newport on the Hereford, Abergavenny and Newport railway line. Approaching Newport, the feted locomotive, King George V, would, much to the chagrin of train-spotters from outside the area, by-pass Newport Railway Station, on a loop line, and continue to Bristol.

Among several things which made this locomotive a star was a silver bell.

Designed and built in 1927 to represent Great Britain and the Great Western Railway at the prestigious Baltimore and Ohio Railroad celebrations, the first of the new King-class locomotives underwent trials before being lifted on the *SS Chicago City* at Roath Dock, Cardiff.

Many thousands of railway enthusiasts attended the American exhibition where King George V became the centre of attraction.

A large oval track with a gentle incline, which ran in front of the main grandstand, allowed spectators to see the locomotives in motion without assisted power. As the new American locomotives rolled past the grandstand, the expected groaning, squeaking and clanking of their progress was deafening to some spectators.

When it became the turn of King George V to parade, Driver W. Young allowed the engine to freewheel down the slope approaching the grandstand.

The British engine moved past the grandstand in complete silence.

It was a full minute before the stunned audience broke into rapturous applause. For its contribution to the proceedings an inscribed silver bell was presented and will still be seen on the buffer-beam at the front of the locomotive.

The Valley boys were privileged to have the King in their area and any father who does not strive today to give his young son the opportunity to see this great locomotive will miss a unique experience.

LEST WE FORGET

s a consequence of the Juvenile Offender's Act of 1854 and the further introduction of the second reading in Parliament of the Reformatory Schools Bill in the summer of 1857, the land was prepared for a number of special schools to be erected in England and Wales.

The criteria for admission to these Reformatory Schools is clearly stated in the Director's Minute Book, which is easily accessible in the Gwent Record Office, Cwmbran. This, now valuable record states that a Reformatory was established for, 'the reception of boys under sixteen years of age convicted of theft and other offences, who appear to have entered upon a course of crime and whom reasonable hope may be entertained of their amendment'.

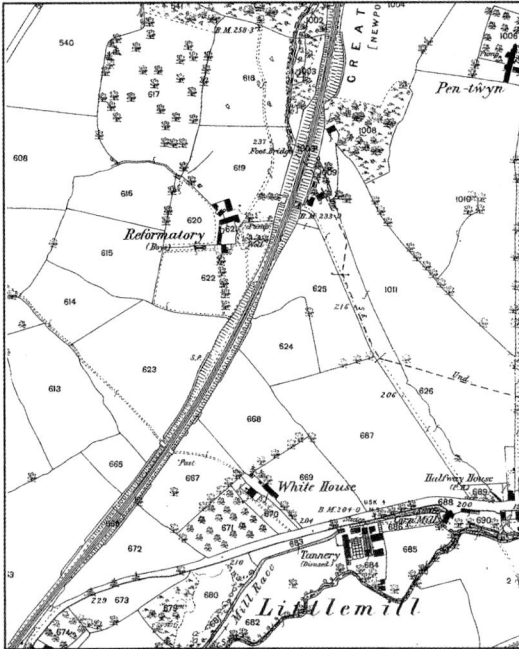

Little Mill Reformatory circa 1880 (from the Ordnance Survey Map)

The Monmouthshire Reformatory at Little Mill was certified to open its doors on February 7th, 1859, and the first three boys entered the institution. In these early days it was the magistrates who decided if an additional reformatory sentence was required after a boy had already completed a period in prison. Life was indeed harsh for these young lads who committed only mi-demeanours, which would be tolerated much more sympathetically today. The regime of the institution remained basically the same as what they would experience in the prison system. In the period 1859-1900, 292 boys aged between eight and fifteen years received reformatory sentences at the Monmouthshire Reformatory ranging from between two and five years.

By the outbreak of World War One the excellent care and attention of the managers and staff of the Reformatory had become widely recognised due to the tremendous beneficial effects in dealing with juvenile crime in the county.

It was in June 1915, when a decision was made that all boys on-licence and suitable to enlist should be allowed to do so. Serving King and country would also influence the time each lad would spend on-licence.

130 boys who had been educated at the Reformatory served in the Great War in either the Army or Navy. A number of them would receive honours and decorations.

On November 22nd, 1915, the Director's Minute Book record the visit to the Little Mill Reformatory school for boys of Corporal Frank Pearce, a former inmate at the institution. As a member of the 1st Battalion, Royal Welsh Fusiliers, he had recently been awarded the Distinguished Conduct Medal for his services at the Front. The official announcement of the medal is as follows:-

> 1077, Private F. Pearce, 1st Battalion, Royal Welsh Fusiliers.
> For conspicuous bravery from September 25th to 29th, 1915, near Hullock. Private Pearce, one of the regimental stretcher bearers, with great heroism, and regardless of all personal danger, brought in wounded men throughout the day and night under heavy and continuous fire, carrying many of them on his back. His bravery and devotion is beyond praise.

The hero of the day received a great ovation from the boys on his arrival and was hospitable entertained by the Superintendent and managers. At the time the lads in the school were engaged in making mailbags for the Government, as well as assisting neighbouring farmers with agricultural work.

As expected there would be fatalities amongst their number and ten boys would not return home from the carnage.

On Saturday 7th, November, 1914, nineteen year old Leonard Walter Oram Head died during military operations in the Ypres Salient. Earlier, on February 6th, 1911, he had been found guilty at Salisbury City Court, of embezzlement, and sentenced to three years. Previous convictions consisted of: wilful damage, stone throwing, stealing a screwdriver, violence, and malicious damage. He had been well treated at home with his father in regular employment as a whipthong maker. His name is to be found on the Ypres (Menin Gate) Memorial, Belgium, where he is remembered with honour.

Pte. Henry V. Winwood, Blaenavon

Henry (Harry) V. Winwood was the son of Emanuel Winwood, a peddler, of Woodland Street, Blaenavon. There was nothing to indicate that this young man would be in dispute with the law during his younger days. Leaving school at an early age, the work at Kays Slope Colliery, Blaenavon, as a haulier, kept his youthful energies very much occupied. However, the later breaking into Westleyan School and stealing therefrom brought him nine strokes of the birch. This was shortly followed by an offence of stealing one gross of shoelaces. For this, the thirteen year old was sentenced to four years at the Little Mill Reformatory.

He readily volunteered for military service at the outbreak of war and soon found himself at Ploegsteert, Belgium, with the 2nd Battalion, Monmouthshire Regiment. A letter sent home in early December informed his mother that he had been in the trenches for 11 days, four in and four out. The Germans were so close that they could throw stones into their trenches. On one occasion, when out of the trenches, a German flare lit up the terrain and he had to immediately jump into a hole to escape being shot. The hole was unexpectantly full of water and covered him up to his chest.

Rumours began to circulate in Blaenavon during Xmas week that the young man had been fatally wounded, but it was not until mid-January that his mother received a letter from the War Office informing of her son's death on December 14th, 1914. The young Blaenavon man did his duty well and died like a hero. He was buried with other Eastern Valley men at Calvaire (Essex) Military Cemetery, Ploegsteert, Belgium, and remembered with honour.

Joseph Byng, 15 years of age, already had a few other minor convictions against him when he was committed at Victoria Courts, Birmingham, for stealing a revolver. The treatment at home by his parents had been good. His time at the Little Mill Reformatory went well and he received good reports while on licence to a farmer in Porthcawl. Immediately his term expired he went to Canada and voluntary letters to Reformatory staff informed them that he had found employment as a timber cutter at 25 dollars a month.

As soon as it was possible the young man became a private in C Co., 1st Battalion, Canadian Infantry (Western Ontario Regiment). Sadly, 6438 Private Joseph Byng, a fit young man who had consciously began to improve his life, died at Ypres on Friday, 23rd April 1915. He is remembered with honour on the Ypres (Menin Gate) Memorial, Belgium.

Another boy came to the Monmouthshire Reformatory from the Victoria Courts, Birmingham. Alfred George Hammond received five years for stealing boots. His home circumstances had been poor but his parents had been good to him. He enlisted on September 18th, 1914 and found himself in 3rd Co., 6th Battalion, South Wales Borderers. Letters to Reformatory staff gave his whereabouts until his obituary was observed in local newspapers. He died on Monday, 8th November 1915. 17571 Private A.G. Hammond is buried and remembered with honour at Bailleul Communal Cemetery Extension, Nord, France.

When only fourteen years old Charles Brown stole 6/- from a gas meter at his home in London. His mother and only parent worked as a boxmaker. He was to stay until 19 years of age in the Little Mill Reformatory. On August 5th, 1915, he enlisted in the Royal Sussex Regiment. Field postcards from the Front kept Reformatory staff aware of his progress. An official communication and a letter from his mother, informed that he had been killed in action on August 16th, 1916.

Richard Henry Curtis had been detained by police for begging in the street and subsequently appeared at the Victoria Court, Birmingham, in June 1912. At the time he was fifteen years of age with no previous convictions. His mother had died and the treatment he received from his father had been good. Unfortunately, as he grew older the lad became beyond control of his father who was 65 years of age. Letters to Reformatory staff told of his progress at the front. Wounded in April 1916, another letter from 3017, Signaller R.H. Curtis, 2nd., Battalion, Royal Warwickshire Regiment, informed that he was going out again. Later reported missing, his father would read out a letter from his commanding officer to Reformatory staff stating that the lad had been killed in action on Sunday, 3rd September 1916. He was buried at Guillemont Road Cemetery, Somme, France, and remembered with honour.

Excitement prevailed at the school when it became known that the brother of a boy on licence and serving at the front had won the Victoria Cross. On behalf of his brother, Sergeant R.J. Bye, VC., of the Welsh Guards, would visit the school to make a presentation.

The conduct of the Reformatory boys serving King and country was exemplary except for one tragic exception. A boy from the school became the victim of the now recognised infamous policy of the army to court martial innocent serving soldiers in what was thought to be an attempt to maintain discipline. The Reformatory lad had enlisted on August 28th, 1914, and did his duty well in India and Mesopotamia before going missing. The managers of the school would receive a letter from the lad's mother with official notification that her son was shot for desertion after trial by Court Martial on 25th July, 1917.

Arthur Pinfield, aged 15 years, also came from the Victoria Law Courts, Birmingham, after being convicted of stealing weaving apparel. He was to serve until nineteen years of age at the Monmouthshire Reformatory. On April 21st, 1917, he enlisted under the Military Service Act and became 65239 Private A. Pinfield, 18th Battalion, Welsh Regiment. Reported missing at first, a later official statement informed the Reformatory that he was killed in action on Saturday, April 13th, 1918.

Edward Percy Robinson, of 6 George Street, Salisbury, came to Monmouthshire from the local Petty Session Court after being convicted of stealing a pair of boots. Admitted on June 21st,1913, he faced three years in the Reformatory. Enlisting in the 1st Battalion, Middlesex Regiment, on September 10th, 1916, he would maintain a high standard with his military duties. An official report received by the Reformatory informed that he had been killed in action at Achion, France, on October 23rd, 1918. A letter at the same time from his mother also informed that he had been "killed in action" and "has been recommended for the Military Cross for conspicuous devotion to duty." Private Robinson is buried and remembered with honour at Croix Churchyard, Nord, France.

Sadly, the details of A. Coombes, the other lad from the Reformatory to die during the Great War is unavailable despite exhaustive searches being made.

41

Hopefully, a young scribe in the future will be successful in revealing how this Reformatory lad is remembered with honour.

The war which was to end all wars at last came to an end. On August 11th, 1919, the boys from the Little Mill Reformatory attended the Peace Celebrations at Mamhilad and Monkswood. It would be on September 13th, 1921, when at a meeting of the Reformatory managers, a resolution was passed to the effect that a brass tablet on a wooden block be obtained to commemorate the names of those boys who were killed or died on active service in the Great War.

It was resolved at a further meeting that the memorial tablet be fixed up in Monkswood Church, where the boys regularly attended.

On the 23rd March, 1922, Monkswood Church became the scene of a simple ceremony in honour of nine boys who had died

Monkswood Church

in the service of their King and country. Headed by their brass band the boys from the Little Mill Reformatory, attired in cadet uniform, marched to the church and took their seats in the choir near the Union Jack which covered the memorial. After a short service the honour of unveiling the memorial fell to Colonel J.A. Bradney,C.B., who spoke highly of the boys from the Little Mill Reformatory school. In his speech he told of the 130 boys who had served in the war with many of them receiving honours and decorations.

Sadly, no mention was made of the young lad shot for desertion and neither was his name entered on the memorial plaque.

The memorable service proved to be one of the last functions of the Little Mill Reformatory school for boys. Owing to the need for economy and in consequence of the falling off in the number of boys sent to such institutions, through the adoption of other means of dealing with juvenile offenders, the Reformatory officially closed its doors in 1922.

To the Glory of God.
AND IN MEMORY OF THE FOLLOWING
BOYS OF THE MONMOUTHSHIRE REFORMATORY
WHO FELL IN THE GREAT WAR, 1914-1918.

BROWN C,	HAMMOND
BYNG J.	HEAD L.W.
COOMBES A.	PINFIELD
CURTIS R.H.	ROBINS
WINWOOD H.	

"Lest we forget"

SIR BRIGGS

t was in 1915 when 'Granny' Catherine Beynon-Rees spoke of the famous Charge of the Light Brigade and remembered that the people of her home town, Tredegar, talked of nothing else for weeks because Godfrey Morgan, of Tredegar House, Newport, had taken part. She remembered the celebrations in the town on his homecoming from the Crimea War and everyone realised how lucky he was when only 195 survived out of the 673 who gallantly started along the Valley of Death.

On that fateful day he sat astride his hunter Sir Briggs, the horse he purchased after watching him win the Hunt Steeple Chase at Cambridge in 1851.

While much has been written about the brave men who took part in the legendary charge, little is recorded of the noble animals who accompanied their masters.

Sir Briggs, wide eyed with fear, carried Captain Morgan along the Valley while men and horses fell dead and dying alongside them. Behind them, and accompanying the 11th Hussars, came another four footed friend, a small terrier dog who went by the name of Jemmy.

Sir Briggs carried his master with the few that remained of the first line to the guns, and it was there that a final salvo caused the frightened horse to turn. Captain Morgan brought Sir Briggs around and put him at it again, and they went passed the guns.

Outnumbered and badly mauled, the only hope of escaping capture was to return along the body strewn valley before the remnants of the Light Brigade became enveloped by the Russians.

Sir Briggs had by this time been struck by the sabre of a mounted gunner, but the wound below the left eye did not slow down the strong horse.

It was a race to get clear before the enemy surrounded them. Captain Morgan struck a Russian as he ran one of his colleagues through with a lance. With the situation becoming even more desperate, the young captain dug his spurs into his horse's side and Sir Briggs went for it as he had often gone at the big fences in Monmouthshire.

As the enemy closed in, Captain Morgan attempted to parry several Cossack lances poking at him, but unfortunately one got through and caused an injury to the groin. Regarded as a minor injury at the time, the wound would be the cause of the likeable young man to never marry or have children.

What was left of the Light Brigade fought their way back along the Valley until they reached safety.

Jemmy was among the survivors. The small dog went passed the guns and although bleeding badly from two wounds in the neck due to shrapnel splinters, the loyal animal would live and return to England.

Sir Briggs came home and lived a good life until he died at Tredegar House, Newport, in 1874, aged 28 years.

At the beginning of a quality tour of Tredegar House, which is very good value for money, Sir Briggs will be seen at the guns in a painting commissioned in 1905, and a photograph shows him in old age with his master.

When completing the tour an invitation is given to see the Cedar Garden. The well-kept garden is enhanced by a magnificent Cedar tree. Nearby, and not realised by many, is a circle of yew bushes which surrounds a large obelisk headstone. The inscribed headstone marks the final resting place of Sir Briggs, an equine hero of Balaclava.

Sir Briggs

44

THE DEPUTY FUEHRER

ronwen Rees-Lewis was in the process of manoeuvring the pram containing her new daughter in the direction of Lower Monk Street, Abergavenny, when into view came the tall man with dark features escorted by three military guards, one of which carried a service revolver. They had met in the same circumstances several times before and on each occasion the man had been full of praise of her little girl's beautiful blonde curls. On this occasion he pulled from his grey-blue flying jacket a wooden toy that he had assembled and presented it to the young mother. Then, the Deputy Fuehrer of the Greater German Reich continued his walk with his escort hurrying along in order to keep up.

Rudolph Hess had come under the hypnotic spell of Adolph Hitler in 1920. A close relationship followed and with his tremendous organising skills, and blind obedience, he was the obvious choice to be the Fuehrer's deputy when he came into power.

By the spring of 1941, Hess had began to lose favour and with Germany about to attack Russia, he quietly contemplated a daring plan which would again put him at the front of his government.

While walking in a garden, he and the Fuehrer were heard discussing a move to appease Britain so that all of the German war effort could be directed at the Soviets. At the conclusion of the meeting Hess remarked that if the plan did not work then he would plead insanity.

Shortly after, Hess climbed into the unarmed silver-grey Messerschmitt 110 and began his dangerous flight to Scotland. On the way the pilot of a lone Spitfire fighter plane spotted him and gave chase. The British pilot reported that due to the superior speed of the Messserschmitt 110, and the evasive action of its pilot, he eventually lost sight of him.

Over a chosen area he bailed out. A farm employee found him and took him into his small whitewashed cottage. Here, he was given a cup of tea while the authorities were informed.

Things then started to go wrong for Hess. No one believed who he was. When Prime Minister Churchill was eventually informed he muttered in disbelief, 'Well Hess or no Hess, I'm off to see the Marx Brothers.'

His plan did not work and in June, 1942, he was transferred to Maindiff Court Military Hospital, Abergavenny, for surveillance.

Later he would write the following about Abergavenny: 'The particular beauty of this area, above all the amazing colour change in the hills and mountains, the ever-changing illumination...The doctors who treated me there were in a human sense

especially nice types. One of them, a highly educated, slight and eccentric fellow, the other a little more robust, also very interesting, with whom I had very intelligent conversations...I took long walks around Abergavenny, and sometimes drives in the area...The people whom I met during my excursions behaved impeccably - with hardly an exception. In the villages and towns which I sometimes walked through the people ran to their doors to see the German who had arrived by parachute, and in many cases they appeared very friendly.'

During one of his many long walks in the nearby countryside, a former guard recalls the warm weather which caused all three to sit down on a grass verge to rest. Both guards were soon sleeping and when they awakened, the German second-in-command had left. Staff at the hospital later observed Hess walking up the long driveway alone. When he reached the main entrance of the hospital, his guards were seen running around the corner and entering the driveway at a fast pace.

Rudolf Hess

Psychiatrist Major Ellis Jones was the robust doctor who conversed well with the Deputy Fuehrer. On October 8th, 1945, Dr Ellis Jones escorted Rudolph Hess to the Nuremburg trial where the German was sentenced to life imprisonment.

Following his retirement and around 1955, Dr Ellis Jones gave many interesting talks throughout the Eastern Valley of Monmouthshire about the stay of the Deputy Fuehrer at Abergavenny.

Rudolph Hess remained loyal to his Fuehrer until he died in Spandau Prison on August 17th, 1987, aged ninety-three years.

A FAITHFUL INMATE

ith the passing of the 1834 Poor Law Amendment Act which provided a Board of Guardians who authorised the building of Workhouses, the needs of the poor, sick and aged within a parish were, to some extent, gradually met.

Due to this new legislation the Union Workhouse at Coedygric, near Pontypool, was erected in 1837.

Short stay or long stay residents at the Workhouse were obliged to carry out some manual work, thus helping to reduce the running costs of the establishment.

It would be around 1852, when a young lad of fifteen years of age entered the doors of this grim building and commenced working for the Workhouse Master. Classified as an 'Idiot,' he would have a unique career which lasted for eighty years.

Although handicapped with a severe speech impediment and incomplete development of intelligence, Tom Dukes soon won the trust of the Master by his enthusiasm to finish any task allocated to him. In particular he could be relied upon to responsibly deliver any message within a wide radius of Griffithstown. It was not long before the tradesmen receiving his master's messages became known to him by a name which referred to their particular line of business.

Another of his traits was the playing of his beloved mouth organ. Often he would be seen around the Pontypool district delivering messages while playing *Three Blind Mice*, the only tune he

Tom Dukes

knew. Children skipped along behind him and remembered the stern warning from their fathers of what would happen to them if they were caught teasing the young man.

He would regularly be seen descending Greenhill Road, Sebastopol, before returning to the Workhouse along Wern Road. If by chance he came across a group of housewives canting on a doorstep, Tom immediately seized the opportunity to beguile the small audience with his musical ability. This would be rewarded by a large slice of home-made cake and Tom never missed calling at the same house to give a musical rendering during subsequent visits to the village.

The years went by and Tom would almost always be included in the official programme for the Christmas concert at the Workhouse. On rare occasions, Tom's

name did not appear in the list of performers. During these performances, the staff at the Coedygric Institution would observe Tom leaving his allocated seat at the back of the hall and gradually move nearer the stage whenever anyone vacated their seat. Within striking distance of the platform and during a lull in the programme, Tom would always bound onto the stage to give his favourite performance. This would be met with loud applause.

If asked about a former Master of the Institution who had been kind to him before sadly committing suicide, Tom would draw a finger across his throat and point to the ground.

His love for flowers knew no bounds and at the end of every week he somehow mysteriously produced a beautiful bunch of flowers for the Matron.

At the age of 95 years he would still be seen shuffling around the district wearing his old 'captain's' cap while delivering messages.

He was on duty until suffering a stroke some three weeks before his death. Never before had there been a funeral at the Institution as the one for Tom Dukes in 1932. A large crowd gathered on the road outside his home for the past eighty years, and, as the cortege moved along Stafford Road, the blinds in every house were drawn as a sign of respect for the much loved old man.

THE LAST OF THE OLD SECOND MONMOUTHSHIRES

orn during the reign of Queen Victoria, at 26, Chapel Lane, Upper Race, near Pontypool, Phillip Morgan celebrated his 101st birthday at the Wentsland Nursing Home, Tranch, Pontypool, on February 13th, 1997.

For his hundredth birthday the staff at the nursing home did him proud. On the auspicious day the veteran soldier received the customary telegram from his monarch and as the day progressed the band of The Royal Regiment of Wales arrived, accompanied by their mascot. Stirring music could be heard during the celebration tea and the festivities continued into the night.

Phillip attended the Race Chapel with his father, a former Gloucestershire farmer. He well remembers setting the hooks in nearby Glyn Brook which ran from the large Glyn Pond. The next morning a good number of hooked fish would be collected for the frying pan.

The Great War commenced and Phillip, aged eighteen years, immediately joined the 2nd Monmouthshires. At the beginning of November, 1914, the regiment arrived at Le Havre on board a cattle boat named the *Manchester Importer*. The young Pontypool man would serve all through the long, terrible war.

It is when talking about the difficult circumstances during this time that his irrepressible humour becomes evident. Of the many terrifying events which he experienced, participation with the famous tunnelling unit quickly came to mind. While the chosen tunnelling unit burrowed beneath the German lines, prior to becoming the first group to blow a large crater in the enemies trenches, Phillip would be busy at the tunnel entrance. His work consisted of removing the large sacks of earth excavated from the tunnel and emptying them on top of the trench.

While clambering with his heavy load to the top of the trench he looked up and observed a large German shell, on that occasion, spiralling in his direction. He dropped on the wet earth and although the large shell passed overhead, he raised his left leg which momentarily came into view of the German snipers and they had him in the ankle. When asked if the injury hurt at the time, Phillip paused and chuckled, "I'm glad it wasn't my head."

Further evidence of accepting what fate had thrown his way emerged when asked if he suffered from frost bite in the wet and muddy trenches. "No" he immediately replied, "I was moving too quick."

Phillip came home and married his childhood sweetheart, the girl who had always lived next door. When asked how he met his wife he smiled again and said, "While playing marbles." After the Great War the young family settled in Crumlin Street, Pontypool, where the veteran would reside for the remainder of his life.

Phillip Morgan 1918

During the Second World War he did Fire Service in Pontypool. A son and daughter were the issue of a happy marriage, but sadly his son, a member of the Welsh Guards, was killed in action.

Most of his working life was spent in the gruelling sheet mills of Panteg Steel Works. Although a keen gardener, his first passion became rugby football and he was for a while, probably, the longest supporter of Pontypool R.F.C.

Never to envy the bravery awards of his comrades and just thankful to have survived the slaughter, Phillip Morgan has deservedly, and without seeking it, found fame as the last soldier of the 2nd Monmouthshire Regiment who fought in The Great War.

Phillip Morgan on his 100th birthday

ABE LINCOLN ARRIVED TOO!

orn 1834, in the parish of Llanfrechfa Upper, and long before the village of Pontnewydd came into being, William Davis would be remembered in the district as 'Yankee' Davis many years after his long life ended.

In search of adventure and employment a young William Davis left home to try his luck in America.

Arriving in a vast land seething with unrest, the young man from the lower reaches of the Eastern Valley of Monmouthshire became caught up in America's most tragic of conflicts.

Receiving pay as a member of the Pennsylvania Cavalry, Trooper Davis fought for the Union cause against the South and witnessed the birth of a new country.

It was a war that tore a nation apart. Brother fought brother, father fought son, and many won the red badge of courage at Bull Run, Shilo, and Gettysburg; to name just a few of the battles where bloody mayhem became part of history.

The four year war was nearly over and Trooper Davis participated in the drive to Richmond, the capital of the Confederacy.

Davis rode into Richmond with his troop only to find most buildings on fire and looted by the retreating Southerners. Orders were given to extinguish the fires and salvage as much of the property as possible.

With the fires under control, it would not be long before President Abraham Lincoln walked through the streets in full view of any lingering snipers.

Headstone of William Davis

Bill Davis had enough adventures to last him several lifetimes and he returned home to marry Hannah Davies, a Pontnewydd girl, in 1867.

An idyllic life followed for the battle hardened veteran as Pontnewydd developed into the village that we know today. Employed in various roles in a local ironworks, he lived for a short period in one of several new houses near Ladywell

Road, Pontnewydd. Known as Richmond Place, a larger building project adjoining the properties soon developed into Richmond Road. Folklore has it that the roads received their names due to the presence of 'Yankee' Davis.

An expert gardener who enjoyed a pipe of tobacco, Bill Davis spent the latter part of his life at Brynhyffryd Place, Croesyceiliog. From here he would walk the short distance to Llanfrechfa Grange and receive his army pension, collected for him at a Newport bank by Mr. A.C. Mitchell, banker, iron master, and Justice of the Peace.

The highly respected old veteran of the American Civil War was buried in the ancient All Saints Church, Llanfrechfa, in 1919. His epitaph reads: "Now the Warrior's task is o'er."

LOST ALBERT MEDAL SEES LIGHT OF DAY

The 1913 Whitsuntide Bank Holiday had arrived and the Blackwood lads were in no doubt about how they intended to enjoy the respite from their dangerous work in Oakdale Colliery.

All were in favour of visiting the annual Pontypool Fete in the new park called the Polo Grounds near Pontypool Road Railway Station.

The well organised excursions to the fete by the Great Western Railway were a sell out. Boisterous travellers looked forward to seeing Frenchman, Mons. Leotana, perform his thrilling tricks on the steel wire at a height far in excess of that achieved by the famous Blondin.

Barely out of his teens, John Cynon Jones, a Blackwood collier, enjoyed the good natured banter of his young colleagues as the crowded train arrived at the old Pontypool Road Station. Unknown to everyone, the most daring act of the holiday period was about to take place.

John Cynon Jones eagerly joined the throng on the station's platform. So did a young lad, also from Blackwood, by the name of Percy Gwilt, but his leaving the railway carriage soon turned into a nightmare.

Missing his footing on the opposite platform, the fifteen year old fell onto

John Cynon Jones

54

Pontypool Road Station

the railway line and into the path of a non-stop express train coming around the bend at speed. With only seconds available, John Cynon Jones leaped onto the track and snatched the boy under his arm. Taking a step forward he found that he could not budge because of the weight of the boy. His only course of action was to lunge backwards into the small space between the railway track and platform wall. Clasping the boy on top of him the space proved barely sufficient, and as the locomotive passed, the Blackwood collier felt the piston graze his cheek.

The crowd on the platform froze in horror as the train thundered along at seventy miles an hour.

In silence the onlookers inched to the edge of the platform fully expecting to see the mutilated bodies of two young people. To their amazement they saw John Cynon Jones getting up and lifting the dazed young lad into concerned outstretched hands.

Urged to follow the policy of informing the railway officials of the incident, the young collier would have none of it and hurried off to catch up with his colleagues.

The adventure did not end there. Older members of the crowd who witnessed the heroic rescue reported the proceedings and the story spread.

At a public meeting subsequently the Blackwood collier was presented with an inscribed silver pocket watch by the trustees of the Carnagie Hero Fund and a money gift from the Divisional Superintendent of the Great Western Railway.

The story was far from over.

Albert Medal

In January 1914, a letter from the Secretary of State informed John that he had been awarded the highest medal available to a civilian and he was to travel to Buckingham Palace to receive his award from The King.

On February 13th, 1914, His Majesty pinned the Albert Medal on the breast of John Cynon Jones and said, "I am very pleased at your gallant act."

(For many years the Albert Medal was the highest civilian award for an heroic act and the criterion adopted had been that the recipient's risk of death had to be greater than his chances of survival. In 1971, it was announced that the Albert Medal would be replaced by the George Cross and the former medal could be exchanged unless the recipients elected to retain their original medals.)

At the age of 32 years, John Cynon Jones vanished from the old Blackwood electoral lists and his trail went cold. Experts who made a study of Albert Medal recipients could not contribute any further than quoting John's entry in The London Gazette on February 24th, 1914. The whereabouts of the Monmouthshire medal was an even greater mystery. Numerous enquiries around the Welsh valleys proved fruitless and further research in London became unproductive.

A chance meeting with an octogenarian in High Street, Blackwood, resulted in the name of a person who might know if any of the Jones family survived.

Fate had taken over. The clear voice of a senior citizen on the other end of the telephone explained that she knew all about John Cynon Jones and the medal and watch were in her possession.

John Cynon Jones AM., served throughout the Great War with the South Wales Borderers and later married a schoolmistress before deciding to live the remainder of his life in Weston-Super-Mare.

The Albert Medal and silver watch lay in a bedroom chest of drawers and had not seen the light of day for many years until my visit soon after the telephone conversation.

Following advice, the inscribed medal and pocket watch, has now been deposited in a bank for safekeeping.

Both might be sold in the future as one item at a long established auction house.

WHEN *PONTYPOOL* MET THE *OSBORNE*

I t had been prosperous few years for the Pontypool Iron and Tin Plate Company and a further increase in trade in 1871 made it necessary to improve their horse-drawn tramway from Pontnewynydd to Pontymoile.

The arrival of the small locomotive *Pontypool* in December 1871, required enlargement of the blind arch beneath the bridge over the Afon Llwyd, leading from the town to Trevethin Church.

With the necessary alterations completed, the route of the smart little locomotive ran from the Osborne Forge, Pontnewynydd, alongside the Afon Llwyd, some distance through a tunnel under the Italian Garden, and eventually entered a tunnel passing under the Newport and Brecon Canal, at Pontymoile, before arriving at the Lower Mill Works.

Public interest was high as the engine puffed up the incline on its first trip. With many of the town's people employed by the Company, their children were full of anticipation for the momentous occasion. When the engine approached the town, a large crowd hurried to catch sight of it and enthusiastic cheers indicated the respect felt for the Iron Company.

It would not be long before another small locomotive, the Osborne, was purchased and also made the picturesque journey on the single line alongside the Afon Llwyd.

With the Company's rule of no more than one engine using the track, everything went well until the summer of 1874. Now we often hear the saying of being in the wrong place at the wrong time and this could not have proved more fatal than on a quiet Saturday afternoon in July.

The *Osborne* with three laden trucks, and in the care of both the driver and traffic manager, had left the Pontnewynydd Works before approaching Pontymoile canal tunnel at full speed. Unknown to them, the *Pontypool* pulling trucks containing tin, was on the south side of the canal with the intention of passing through the thirty metre tunnel, on its way to the sidings at Pontypool Road.

As usual, John Jones, the driver of *Pontypool*, pulled up near the tunnel entrance and operated the engine's whistle. Having given a warning and everything appearing satisfactory, he proceeded slowly with his fireman, John Morgan, in attendance.

When the interior of the tunnel came into view, John Jones was astonished to see the *Osborne* in the tunnel and coming through at great speed. He sounded the whistle and with his fireman, jumped for his life.

When the *Osborne* hit the *Pontypool* it sounded like a clap of thunder which was heard for a long distance.

'Pontypool' locomotive - property of Pontypool Iron & Tinplate Co.

People came running from every direction. Jones and Morgan, saved only by their quick action, picked themselves up from the floor unhurt.

Reuben Lidington, the driver of the *Osborne*, clambered off the engine with difficulty, his leg badly damaged.

The traffic manager, Alfred Robinson had not been so fortunate. Suffering badly with internal injuries, he was placed on a wooden door and carried to his lodgings at Clarence Street. With Dr Essex in attendance, the mournful procession approached the Clarence Hotel when Robinson put out his hand to one of the bearers, and said, "I am dying!" His life was then snuffed out.

The small locomotives continued along their scenic route for many years, but the ghost of Alfred Robinson haunted the Pontymoile tunnel until the line closed. On a quiet summer night, towpath walkers, if they listen intently, might still hear the rumblings of these old servants of the iron road.

A FIRST FOR TALYWAIN

I n 1908, the Territorial Army came into existence with the aim of becoming more efficient than the old Volunteer Force which it replaced. Four years later, a young Bert Pinchin, of 1, Emlyn Terrace, Talywain, became a part-time soldier in the 2nd Battalion, The Monmouthshire Regiment, and accepted the obligation to turn out for the defence of his country when required.

Life for the eighteen year old didn't offer very much while employed as a collier at the nearby Blaensychan Colliery. His father carried on the business of an upholsterer and French polisher, while his grandmother was the licensee of the popular Winning Horse Public House, Pontypool.

Following two years part-time military experience he was one of the earliest to volunteer for active service at the outbreak of World War One.

Little did he know that it would only be a short while before his small sister, Emily, had occasion to excitedly call him from his bed to hear his fellow Territorials giving him three cheers as they marched past the family home in Talywain.

Promotion to Corporal came quickly on the French battlefields and on December 8th, 1914, Bert deservedly won a unique honour when he became the first member of the Territorial Army to win a medal. When interviewed about his commendable behaviour, the modest young man, who thought he had only done his duty, gave the following account:

> "My section was working down the left end of our regiment. I had been continually warning the men not to go across some open ground for wood, as we would get the German snipers at the barn. At last, about 3 o'clock, about twenty men crossed over, and as I expected, the snipers fired at the barn. Lance Corporal Prince and Private Davies were wounded. The former managed to get back, but Davies was dying. I was instructed to go across and get him from there. He was in a dying condition. Sergeant Coombes was with him and between us we did our best for him, but he died trying to say something. We could not make out what he said. Another man, named Private Roberts, was also wounded, and as Private Davies was dead I left him to attend to Private Roberts. When going across to the barn I got hit, and was wounded in the right arm, so that I only had one arm free to work upon both Davies and Roberts. I bandaged Roberts up and carried him to a place of safety. I stayed with him until night, as it was not safe to shift by day. After leaving him in safety I went to see to my own wound. I think Sergeant Coombes acted bravely."

For his gallant act Corporal A.E. Pinchin received the Distinguished Conduct Medal.

Albert Pinchin, DCM

While on leave in 1915, Mrs W.P. James presented the young man with a gold watch in the Co-operative Hall as his older brother Fred Pinchin, who would win the Military Medal with the Rifle Brigade, looked on approvingly.

A.E. Pinchin, D.C.M., survived the war to marry and live most of his life in Newport. From here he attended many parades. He retired from his employment as an electrical engineer and later moved to Cardiff where he died in October 1963, aged 66 years.

His unique achievement is recorded for posterity in the published history of the 2nd Battalion, The Monmouthshire Regiment. Perhaps one day the exclusive medal will be placed in the Regiment's museum at Brecon for all to see.

THE LONGEST SIX IN THE VALLEY

rthur Johnston, of Cwmbran, came from impeccable sporting stock. His father was Frank H. Johnston, a triple Welsh champion half-miler and a participant in the famous Powderhall sprint race. Brothers, Mel and Frank, were to become well known local sportsmen, but it would be Arthur who was to receive fame for all time as the man who hit the longest six in the Eastern Valley of Monmouthshire.

In the early 1930's, Arthur took up the same occupation as his father. Employed as an operator of a nut cutting machine in Guest, Keen and Nettlefolds Works, Cwmbran, Arthur was introduced to the sporting side of the large works by his father, who also coached the renowned Cwmbran Harriers.

Unharnessed, Arthur's talent on the cricket field was allowed to grow and not long after he came to the notice of the now famous Glamorgan County Cricket Club.

This was a time when the county cricket team consisted of Players and Gentlemen. Players were only allowed to address a Gentleman member of the same team with the title Mr., and both groups of players used separate dressing rooms. The opportunity to play for the county team came about not by talent alone, but also due to a well-to-do social background.

Every two years, Glamorgan C.C.C. played a local side with the aim of looking for talent and it was the turn of Cwmbran Cricket Club to be thrashed by the senior side.

Arthur Johnson

That day everything went well for Arthur on the playing field. Although on the losing side, the slim young man bowled well, taking three wickets, before becoming Cwmbran's highest run maker.

Later in the afternoon he was interviewed by Maurice Turnbull, a county player and later secretary of the club. Everything appeared amicable to young Arthur until asked what his father's occupation was. "He operates a bolt cutting machine in the

local iron works, Sir" answered Arthur respectfully. Mr. Turnbull closed his notebook and Arthur was left to reflect what might have been.

Arthur continued to mature as a cricket player and became a sporting hero in his district.

It was on a sunny Saturday afternoon when Arthur performed a feat which was destined to be remembered in perpetuity. With times very hard and not much money about, a cricket match, including a break for cucumber sandwiches, was a pleasant way for everyone to enjoy the fine weather.

Already on a high score, a loose delivery came down the wicket and Arthur gave the new ball a tremendous clout. The ball seemed to go on for ever, over the heads of the spectators sitting alongside the boundary line and onto the distant railway embankment. The ball, obscured by a passing train carrying fine coal from Blaenavon, had definitely been hit for a six and the applaud could be heard around the ground.

Funds were short at the Cwmbran club making it necessary to quickly find the ball. Everyone looked but to no avail. Someone remembered the passing coal train and suggested ringing the office of the railway company. Immediately a company official instigated a search for the ball. It would be the next day, at Cardiff Docks, that a vigilant railway employee spotted the ball on the top of a coal truck and about to be tipped into the hold of a ship bound for foreign parts.

Few braver or better men could have put bat to ball than Arthur Johnston on that sunny afternoon, long ago.

THE MAN WHO SAVED WALES

rising early from bed on a misty December morning, many Pontypool townsmen quickly connected with their work boots in the hope of an early start to the 15 miles trek to the Arms Park, Cardiff. Here they would meet other Monmouthshire men having to use the same means of transport due to strike conditions. It was all worth it by the end of that particular afternoon in 1905, for they had been there to see rugby history being made.

At 101 years of age, Phillip Morgan, of Pontypool, remembers the day clearly, he was almost there. Phillip was a dedicated rugby fan all his long life. When only a small lad he would eagerly clean his older brother's best shoes before receiving payment of three pennies for the task.

Tuppence of this would be spent entering the Recreational Ground to watch Pontypool RFC play and one penny would go to a vendor outside the ground for the purchase of a bag of bullseyes. It would be the closest the young lad ever got to heaven.

Phillip's hero, Cliff Pritchard, would later live only a few doors away in Crumlin Street.

C.C. Pritchard had already won two Welsh caps and this heavy, hard tackling centre from Pontypool would win the third of his five caps as 'extra back' against an invincible All Blacks side.

47,000 spectators saw the Welshmen run onto the field; a striking contrast in their scarlet jerseys to the sombre black of the New Zealanders. The visitors strange war dance preceded the Welsh national anthem. As the haunting melody of 'Hen Wlad Fy Nhadau' sounded, for the very first time, the players were seen to be reverently singing. The crowd seeing this and sensing the occasion, became one voice.

Cliff Pritchard tackled like he had never done before and destroyed the New Zealanders. On one occasion only the Pontypool man stood between the Welsh try-line and the huge All Black centre three-quarter R.B. Deans. Cliff brought him down with a crunching tackle.

Pritchard, the son of a Pontypool undertaker, had been laying out the men in black for well into the first half when a scrum inside New Zealand twenty-five would

bring the only score of the game. The Welsh scrumhalf opted to attack on the blind side of the scrum only to see the All Black defence quickly alert to the danger. A change of direction to the open side preceded a long pass which Cliff Pritchard skilfully picked off his boot laces. The game was won with that acrobatic feat. Finally receiving the ball, Morgan, the little Welsh left-wing scored wide out and the prolonged pandemonium caused a cart-horse to bolt down Westgate Street. Inspired by the example of tackling by the Pontypool man, all the Welsh team defended magnificently for the remainder of the game and the final result was a 3-0 win for Wales. Sadly, a disputed New Zealand try, (when Bob Deans tried to wriggle over the try-line) became the talking point of the match and C.C. Pritchard never fully received the just recognition for the part he played in that great game.

With the game won and history made, the celebrations began. A telegram to Pontypool giving notice of the famous result caused a young boy, who had almost made the trip, to jump with joy.

It had been a long day for Cliff Pritchard. Exhausted, he climbed on the last train to leave Newport Station bound for the Eastern Valley. Everything could wait until tomorrow was his only thought as he alighted onto the Pontypool railway platform.

Within seconds he was surrounded by hundreds of Pontypool well-wishers. A young Phillip Morgan would never forget being part of the procession which carried the Welsh hero shoulder high to his home in Crumlin Street.

TRAGEDY BENEATH THE WAVES

n all probability Jocelyn Alfred Millard became the Eastern Valley's first sub-mariner. The youngest son of Mr and Mrs George Millard, of Iona House, Garndiffaith, he attended the West Monmouthshire School before entering H.M. Royal Navy in 1911. In October 1913, the Garndiffaith man volunteered for the new and dangerous submarine service.

At that time submarine warfare was in its infancy with much still to be learned. Underwater craft were slow with control difficult, and the brave men who added to the science of these strange shaped vessels were indeed a rare breed.

Always interested in things of a mechanical nature, it was natural for the young man to attain the position of engine room artificer.

Only just married, the outbreak of the Great War disrupted his life, but with a brother at the time serving with the army in India, he was also ready to do his duty.

On board the submarine E4 off the coast of Harwich, it would be a day of exercises for the Eastern Valley man during August 1916. Another submarine, the E41, served as a surface target ship while the submarines E31 and E4, the latter commanded by Lt-Commander Julian Tenison, commenced a sham attack.

As the day was clear with good visibility, both attacking submarines had no difficulty in holding a steady depth or observing the E41 through their respective periscopes.

Mr Jocelyn A. Millard E.R.A., R.N.

When completing their attack, both submarines came to the surface.

A signal informing that another submarine had been delayed caused a change in the planned training programme and it was decided that the E41 would continue to serve as a target vessel by approaching from a different direction.

The scene was set for a disaster which claimed the lives of forty-five seamen.

The target vessel lookout observed the E31 periscope for some time after it had dived, but of the E4 he saw nothing until the sudden appearance of its periscope only fifty yards off his bow.

The Submarine E4 outward bound on a glassy sea

They were on a collision course. The E4 struck the E41 around 25 feet forward of its conning tower.

The E4 containing Jocelyn Alfred Millard went straight to the bottom of the sea.

Ninety seconds later the E41 went down with only twenty men clearing the hatches in time.

Hopes of further survivors were on the wane when after an hour and thirty minutes Stoker William Brown came to the surface having escaped via the engine room hatch.

A few days later both submarines were raised and put back into service.

Mr Jocelyn A. Millard, E.R.A., R.N., was laid to rest in the Submarine Enclosure, St. Mary's Church, Shotly, not far from Harwich. Here, an impressive stone memorial to the men who died in the E4 incident was visited by a young wife and two small children who were left to mourn their loss.

INTO THE JET AGE

O n Armistice Day, the smart young men of the Cwmbran Air Training Corps always add to the dignity to the proceedings as they stand in echelon near one of the district's war memorials.

The fathers of these lads in blue were young men themselves when a man from their valley stood before the Queen to receive the coveted Air Force Cross.

Born in 1922, John Rees remains today a worthy role-model for any youth wishing to take up a career in the Royal Air Force.

The third son of Mr H. Rees, a collier, of Davies Court, Garndiffaith, he attended the Garndiffaith and Abersychan Grammar Schools. Leaving school at 14 years of age, an entry examination taken in Newport preceded a three year apprenticeship with the Royal Air Force at Halton.

With the outbreak of war in 1939 he was posted to St. Athan and later to Canada and America, where he qualified as a pilot. For the greater part of the war he served with a photograph reconnaissance unit in the Middle and Far East, before returning to Britain in 1947.

Later in his career he became a senior instructor teaching personnel how to become instructors of those wishing to fly aircraft.

A prodigious career move came when he was asked to join an elite research and development squadron. As a test pilot in the new jet age, one of his many risky tasks was to fly the large, untested Valiant 4 jet bomber.

Vickers Valiant BK Mk1XD823

In 1955 he received the notable Queen's commendation for valuable service in the air and the following year he was informed that he would be the recipient of the Air Force Cross. The Cross was awarded for meritorious service and displaying outstanding courage in the air when not on active service against the enemy.

John, who retired in 1977, continues to live happily with his wife Isobel in Bournemouth. Every Xmas he visits relatives in the Eastern Valley and never fails to look in on his former 92 year old schoolteacher, Gwyneth Wilcox.

HEROISM IN A VALLEY MINE

amuel Williams was every inch a valley man. Although not young, he lived life to the full. A senior fireman at Messrs Vipond's Lower Varteg Colliery for twenty years, his leisure time was spent as a member of the Garndiffaith Welfare Club Committee and bowls club. A skilful bowler he had represented Monmouthshire in the sport. For eleven years he had been a member of Garndiffaith Band with some time spent as their chairman. His two sons had done well for themselves with Edwin a member of Birmingham Police Force, and Leslie, a foreman in a London factory.

Just prior to 1940, Sam had two impressive red brick houses built at the southern entrance to Bailey Road, Garndiffaith, and with his brother Edwin residing next door, the popular collier had everything to live for.

It was a bright, warm day as the big man set off for the colliery with snap box under his arm. The day appeared like any other summer day and August 13th, 1940, gave no sign of foreboding.

Underground, Sam was about his duty of making safety checks when he witnessed a roof collapsing on top of two men. With nobody nearby, and without thought for his personal safety, he went to the aid of the buried men. Finding one man already dead, he gave all his efforts to clearing the debris from the other.

Arthur Jones, a borer, seemed lifeless. With bits of the ceiling still falling, Sam worked his way through to Jones before forcing his hands under him and pulling his prostrate body through the fall.

There was no response from the Talywain collier and with great difficulty Sam lifted his face to the air and revived him.

Help had not yet arrived. Jones, now aware of his situation, whispered, "There's some more coming Sam, save yourself."

Another fall came. A large piece of coal hit Sam on the back as he crouched over his partly buried colleague. While still protecting Jones with his body, all he could do was to keep the injured man's airway clear until help arrived.

Both survived and tributes were paid to Sam William's bravery. At a presentation in the Ambulance Hall, Pontypool, the Garndiffaith man received the Carnegie Hero Fund Award.

When asked why he had risked his life, Sam Williams replied, "If you are a Christian, then that is expected of you."

CHRISTMAS DAY IN THE WORKHOUSE

hristmastide in the Coedygric Workhouse at the end of 1897 undoubtedly created problems for its Board of Guardians.

Firstly, they had to put out a statement brought about by a particularly malicious letter received by them concerning the new Workhouse Master. Investigations had proven that there was not a shadow of truth in the suggestion that Mr Richards was frequently from the House and spent his time in low places at Pontypool.

Secondly, with the festive season rapidly approaching, they had to appoint a new cook. Three ladies attended the interview for the responsible post and with the thoughts of the Guardians fixed on the Christmas celebration, each in turn were asked about their competence while cooking plum pudding.

Miss Kate Williams, of Abergavenny, was appointed to the position of cook on a salary of £25 per annum, plus rations, washing and residency at the Workhouse, but without beer.

With funds always extremely short through no fault of the Board of Guardians, the workhouse staff had to use their initiative while applying the traditional decorations to the large house. Holly, mistletoe, ivy and other evergreens were collected by inmates from the nearby canal towpath. In the new infirmary it proved to be a particularly busy period of the year, yet both night nurses found time to make the wards look cheerful for the elderly infirm.

Late on the eve of Christmas, a heavy snowstorm arrived unannounced in Pontypool and the surrounding district.

On Christmas morning the inmates were astir early in anticipation of their annual fare. Breakfast consisted of coffee and bread and butter. Immediately afterwards the men were given an additional allowance of tobacco; whilst the women who required snuff were given the same, and the children received one orange each.

The highlight of the special day would be Christmas dinner in the dinning-hall. In that bygone year the fare consisted of roast beef, boiled potatoes, parsnips and swedes, followed by plum pudding. Several visiting Guardians sampled the prime quality beef and found it well roasted. The plum pudding they found absolutely toothsome.

In place of the usual afternoon meal of bread, butter and jam, tea and Christmas cake were given.

As Christmas night arrived, everyone unanimously agreed that the cooking was excellent and young Miss Williams would be valued by the inmates for many years to follow.

Great credit would also go to Mr Richards while experiencing his first Christmas as Workhouse Master. With only limited resources, he strove hard to see that the needs of 226 inmates under his charge were met on that merry day just over a century ago.

THE PEOPLE'S RECTOR

everend Albert W. Adams-Williams won the hearts of his parishioners whether it was in the sick room, the home, the House of God, or on the roadside. More than that, he would climb down from his horse, pull off his coat, and help any workmen in whatever unpleasant task they were engaged in.

The Rector came from a notable old Monmouthshire family going back hundreds of years. He was entered to the hounds at an early age and as a sportsman in later years it became very hard to follow him when the hounds were in full cry.

The Panteg Rectory always carried big traditions requiring the incumbency to be filled by men of great learning and standing in the Church. It was to this position in the large scattered parish that he succeeded to in 1896.

Famed for his long ponderous speeches and somewhat dashing figure, he remained a bachelor all his life, although many ladies had hopes. A rumour in the hunting field came to nothing, but a passing friendship with a German governess who was at Park House with Squire Hanbury's children, ended in unusual circumstances. The Rector's father was at the time the agent to the Park Estate, and the Rector became a regular visitor there, seeing the children in the schoolroom. One can well understand his courteous manner being misunderstood, and the governess taking his pleasant attentions to her as something more serious. Things reached a climax when she wrote and threatened to throw herself before the altar at a certain evening service. The sidesmen were informed before turning up in force at the service, and sure enough, the

Memorial to
Rev. A.W. Adams-Williams

74

lady rose and proceeded down the aisle. Within metres of the high altar she was met by the sidesmen who firmly escorted her out of the church. The service continued without interruption. Needless to say the governess soon vanished from the Park House.

At the start of the Great War, Rev. Adams-Williams encouraged the young men from his parish to offer themselves for King and country, and cheered them when they were at the front with his letters and spirited verse. While home on leave all the young men would be invited to tea at the Rectory, thus giving the Rector the chance to ask about conditions at the front.

Alas, the war was to take a great toll on the Rector, particularly the May 8th, 1915, action, which claimed the lives of so many boys from his parish and seemed just unbelievable to him.

He died in 1920. His memorial is a tall Celtic cross donated by grateful parishioners. This is to be seen near the entrance of the beautiful old Panteg Church.

BLAENAVON AIRPORT

 ittle Flo put her fingers in her ears as the monster continually roared over her home in Castle Street, Blaenavon. Only nine years of age, she had not seen an aeroplane before. As a matter of fact, very few of the Blaenavon residents had seen one either. The soldiers who returned a year earlier from the Great War witnessed these new machines as they flew over the trenches, but the age of the aeroplane had yet to reach the mountainous town.

Florence Brown remembers waving to the pilot as he slightly banked his aircraft while straining to see a suitable place to land.

Fuel was getting short and he was lost. Hayman's field, Forgeside, appeared to be his best bet to put down and he went for it.

By this time it appeared to Flo that all of Blaenavon were on their doorsteps to see the drama unfolding. In no time the biplane gently descended until it bounced its way along the field behind the former Allgood Avenue.

Hundreds of Blaenavon folk hurried to the spectacle that had never been seen before in the town. Although unable to speak English or Welsh, somehow the pilot managed to explain that he thought he had landed in Abergavenny.

Subsequent events would also convince young Flo of her extended knowledge of aviation.

Several years later a much publicised aerobatics display for the town's people of nearby Abergavenny came to the notice of the astute Blaenavon folk. On a warm afternoon almost the whole population of Blaenavon trekked across the moorland of the Blorenge mountain until they reached the escarpment from which they could see Abergavenny in miniature below.

Flo and her father settled down to wait in anticipation of the unusual entertainment. Soon, the air display began. Whilst the folk of Abergavenny craned their necks upwards to see this new form of entertainment, it seemed to the Blaenavon children that they had to only reach out to touch the now familiar machine as it looped and dived. It would be a rare experience to treasure as children and adults watched at eye level while the aeroplane went through its spectacular routine.

Now 85 years of age, Florence Brown has much to tell of the old days in Blaenavon and her meeting with the famous aviator, Amy Johnson, who toured the Eastern Valley, is a story well worth hearing.

FAITH, HOPE AND CHARITY

he year was 1913 and the war clouds had not yet gathered. Miss Ritchie, matron of Pontypool Hospital, began another busy day organising the work so necessary to relieve pain and give comfort to the patients in her charge. Her close friend, Sister Roots, had difficulty keeping up with her boundless energy as both went about their duties. Soon they would be informed that Dr O'Keefe, a member of the medical staff, would not be visiting the hospital that day due to the untimely death of his wife.

Dr John O'Keefe, had married the daughter of Henry Griffiths, the founder of Griffithstown, some years before and both lived happily at Glengariff, Griffithstown, while watching their two daughters grow up.

The Great War began. Dr O'Keefe and Sarah Ritchie immersed themselves in the extra work the destructive war had caused. A solid working relationship between the couple over many years would in time turn to friendship away from the hospital.

Not wishing her close friendship with Dr O'Keefe to be the cause of broken rules or loss of hospital etiquette, Miss Ritchie resigned from her post of Matron on August 1st, 1915. Although sad to give up her post she was pleased to see her friend, Sister Roots, promoted to Matron.

The great battles abroad resulted in enormous casualties arriving in Britain. Following a quiet marriage at St Mary's Church, Acton, in November, 1915, both Dr O'Keefe and the former Miss Ritchie tackled the huge work load then present in the Griffithstown area.

The Royal Red Cross

Extra to his many medical duties Dr O'Keefe had the responsibility of the two temporary military hospitals in Griffithstown, whilst Mrs O'Keefe exhausted herself as commandant of Panteg V.A.D., and as Matron of Baldwin's Military Hospital.

With the war over and life returning to normal for some, Mrs O'Keefe, as a member of the Territorial Force Nursing Services, received notice that she had been awarded the Royal Red Cross (First Class).

This rare and highly regarded British Military Order consists of an attractive gold cross with red enamel. 'Faith, Hope, Charity' are engraved on the arms of the cross with the date of institution, 1883.

Sadly, her visit to Buckingham Palace would be postponed due to the death of her husband at the end of April, 1919.

It would be in June 1920, when Mrs O'Keefe was received by Queen Alexandra at Marlborough House. Here, she was presented with a book and a signed engraving which showed the Queen's portrait.

Later in the morning the King held an investiture in the Quadrangle of Buckingham Palace, during which he presented the Royal Red Cross to the former Matron of Pontypool Hospital.

Shortly after, Sarah Emily O'Keefe, RRC., left the Eastern Valley forever.

MIDDLE FARM

ocal people welcomed the news that Middle Farm, Stafford Road, Griffithstown, had become a listed building. The ancient 17th century farmhouse received its name because of its middle position in a line of ancient farms beginning with Coedygric Farm on the south side and a Race farm to the north.

Built probably in the second half of the 17th century, little changed until the coming of the railways which caused the muddy highway to be transferred to the back of the premises. This gave access to the public of a 'spout' which had served the farm for several centuries. On a hot day many weary travellers would quench their thirst with the deliciously cold, clear water which had run below ground level down the Penyrheol mountainside. The medicinal properties of this spring water was at one time well known causing people to arrive from far and wide to bottle the mysterious liquid. People living nearby would even limp to the spout and bathe their sprained ankles! Water from the spout was still used by the occupants of the farm until 1956, then the Council provided a cold water tap inside the premises.

Middle farm, Griffithstown

Thomas Stone occupied the farm in 1892 and eventually bought the homestead for £300 in 1922. His granddaughter, Majorie Stone, is the present owner. Previously the farm had been much larger and divided into two living accommodations. With time, the adjoining premises became worn out and had to be demolished.

The building has many architectural features of historical importance and each of the charming bedrooms still has its beams, its window-seat, and view, sweeping from the Pontypool Park to Christchurch and beyond. The roof now consists of artificial stone slate, with much of the original stone roof to be found serving as edging material for a well-tended flower garden.

In 1972, local residents became understandably angry when workmen on a new housing site above Stafford Road covered the spout with a corrugated tin sheet and several tons of earth. The people of Stafford Road sent a petition to Pontypool Council to have their spout exhumed and thanks to the timely intervention of Pontypool Park Estate, the lost water source became available to the community again.

Due to the forward looking attitude of Torfaen County Borough Council, and the expertise of Cadw, many future generations of people will have the opportunity to enjoy this picturesque dwelling when passing.

SECONDS FROM OBLIVION

Due to lack of employment, 1926 was not a good year for Reg Stone. Born on May 16th, 1909, near Big Pond, British, Pontypool, Reg became one of six children who were the issue of a happy marriage between Sam Stone, colliery winding engineman, and his wife Phillipa.

By the time he reached his seventeenth birthday it had become apparent to the young collier that he would have to seek employment away from home due to the General Strike.

Working for a while as an itinerant, he eventually found a permanent job at the Old Kent Road gas works in London. Here he met a young nurse employed at Guy's Hospital and both settled down to married life.

World War Two began and was shortly followed by the dreadful Blitz. Reg, aged 31 years, immediately volunteered for Home Guard duty and became a member of a rescue squad.

Several daring acts of bravery by the Eastern Valley man went unnoticed but it would be at the beginning of 1941 when he caught the eye of the authorities.

Returning to London after leaving his wife and children in the safety of his brother's home in Pontnewynydd, he joined with others in showing the spirit which set an example for the rest of the war effort.

In the early hours of a February morning the capital city was on the receiving end of a particularly heavy bombing raid. Although off duty, Reg immediately joined in the rescue work.

Nearby, a destructive weapon recently produced by the Germans fell in a cluster. These incendiary bombs had warheads of magnesium which burnt so hot that they melted through steel.

Two fell on top of several large gas holders and the whole district was in great danger. In blackout conditions and with hostile planes still bombing in the vicinity, Reg quickly climbed the ladder attached to the side the side of the 90 ft. gas holder. When on top of the large holder, he used his shoe to scoop the deadly burning devise into his helmet before throwing the lot to a safe area on the ground. Looking across, he observed another incendiary bomb on the roof of the adjacent gas holder and although two collegues were trying their best to cope with the dangerous situation, they weren't having much luck.

Reg had received some training in how to deal with the situation. By the time he joined his collegues, a hole had already appeared in the crown of the second gas holder and under pressure, a hissing gas flame of about 10ft was escaping. With only seconds available before the whole district became a mass of flames, he threw a clay pad over the hole and sealed it with wet clay and by emptying sandbags.

Reginald Stone, GM

A modest hero, Reg did not think the deed important enough to inform his wife in Pontnewynydd. It was left to his brother John to spot the report of his brave actions in a national newspaper before informing the rest of the family.

Later, the determined young man would be summoned before the directors of the gas company and thanked for his quick action.

The matter did not end there.

Reginald Stone received notification that for his act of great bravery he would be called to Buckingham Palace to receive the George Medal from King George VI.

The George Medal holder returned to the Eastern Valley in 1947, and most of the remainder of his working life was spent as a collier at the Tirpentwys and Hafodyrynys Colleries.

This popular hero of the Easter Valley lived in Trevethin and was a regular visitor to the Masons Arms Public House, where he took on all challengers at the game of cribbage.

Buried in August 1991, at the ancient Trevethin Church, a simple, small wooden cross marks the final resting place of Reginald Stone, GM. Mr Keith Stone, of Pontypool, hopes one day to put his father's coveted medal on show for all to see in the medal room at the National Museum of Wales.

WHO BLEW THE BUGLE?

s with most disasters it appears that the brave Charge of the Light Brigade was the result of a series of errors. Lord Raglan, commander-in-chief of the British force expected nothing else than to be held accountable. Because of this, in all probability, this good and kind man gave up the ghost in the Crimea and his body would make the long sea journey for burial in Great Britain.

With history always regarded as a controversial subject, the famous charge continues to be a much debated event. A puzzle which intrigues many historians is the unresolved question of who blew the bugle which commenced the charge?

Some experts maintain that the 673 men of the Light Brigade were so in tune with each other that they mounted their horses and moved off without the customary bugle call. Subsequently, these men, who knew they would probably take part in only one cavalry charge in their life-time, and with adrenaline flowing excessively, supposedly changed their horses from the walk to the trot as if by mental telepathy.

Then came the charge. For around 600 men under fire and amid tremendous noise, to suddenly, in unison, change to the charge situation without the sound of one or several bugle calls seems to defy all logic.

On the field of war that day the Light Brigade was divided into three companies, with two platoons to each company. Each platoon had its own bugler, making six in all.

Regretfully, after any major historical event, embellishments, petty jealousies and poor memories, all cause a distortion of the true facts.

W.H. Pennington, who took part in the famous charge and generally sounded the trumpet charge at the Balaclava remembrance day in London, stated that the Brigade moved off on a verbal order with no trumpet note being heard on that day.

If this basic and vital manoeuvre was neglected, then the competence of the commander of the Light Brigade, Lord Cardigan, would have been further seriously questioned. Lord Cardigan (57) although thought to be a thoroughly disagreeable chap, led his men past the Russian guns and having done his job, retired at a walk back along the valley amid the carnage.

Alexander Sutherland (87) while living in retirement in Denver, United States, insisted upon being credited with the honour of blowing the bugle that started the Light Brigade on its tragic journey.

Sutherland maintains that he was only a few yards away from Lord Cardigan when he turned and ordered him to sound the 'attention' and then the 'mount.' Following, and in the right order, he was instructed to blow the 'forward' and the 'trot.' Next, amid the hell taking place, Lord Cardigan calmly turned in his saddle and shouted to Sutherland, 'Trumpeter, sound the charge!'

Charge of the Light Brigade

Among the gallant 673 on that fateful day was Godfrey Morgan (Viscount Tredegar) of Tredegar House, Newport. Although wounded, he survived and received a heroes welcome when he reached Tredegar Park on Wednesday, April 18th, 1855.

The difficult war in the Crimea ended in 1856 and the participants began to put their souvenirs on display.

A sale at a famous London auction house not long after the Crimea War caused something of a stir among military people. Included in the catalogue would be the bugle reckoned to have sounded the charge of the Light Brigade.

Godfrey Morgan, son of Sir Charles Morgan, of Newport, instructed an agent to bid for the unique musical instrument and to offer up to 20 guineas.

It was at this time the dispute began as to whether or not a bugle actually sounded on that eventful day.

The bugle sold for 700 guineas. Godfrey Morgan, became aware of the new controversy surrounding the bugle, and of the meagre sum he said he put up for its purchase. Due to these circumstances, he would tell of his embarrassment caused by the auction for the remainder of his life.

Did the bugle sound on that historic day at Balaclava? The individual is left to make up his own mind, but, old and long-gone Newport historians whispered that the mysterious object on the inventory list of valuables of the Morgan family is the bugle which sounded the charge of the Light Brigade.

SURVIVAL at ARNHEM

aratrooper 4077637 William Farr hit the ground with a jarring thud, but was relieved that no bones had been broken. The descent had been uneventful, not like the frightening landing on the side of Mt. Etna, Sicily. On that occasion he had to use all his nerve to guide the parachute away from the smoke and fumes billowing out of the active volcano. Some of his comrades on that day were not so lucky.

Others members of the 3rd Battalion, Parachute Regiment, soon became organised by finding their companies before commencing the long trek to the Arnhem bridge. All were part of the ambitious plan to quickly capture the large bridge intact, thus making it easier for the allies to enter Germany and bring the Second World War to a close.

Billy Farr had been born in Cwmbran and brought up mainly by an older sister following the death of his mother at an early age. After attending the Catholic School in the ancient village, he immediately volunteered to serve with the Monmouthshire Regiment when war broke out. It was while serving in Northern Island that the Cwmbran lad heard of the need for volunteers for the parachute regiment. He transferred and, as one of the Red Devils, would parachute into North Africa, Sicily and Italy.

Silently the allies entered the town of Arnhem. One of the first half dozen men inside Arnhem would be Vic Williams, who lived opposite the Waterloo Public House, Sebastopol. As soon as the fighting began, the house where Vic had taken cover was hit by a shell. A serious injury to the foot of the Sebastopol man ended a promising career as a football player.

Private Billy Farr played his full part in the fighting for the possession of the bridge as the allied forces hung on grimly while waiting for the promised reinforcements, which never arrived.

Due to overwhelming odds, what was left of the allies were forced to withdraw across the Rhine river by whatever means possible.

Billy Farr, with his friend Private Connolly, gave covering fire while the retreat took place and then had to fend for themselves. With the Germans in hot pursuit both decided to separate and ran up different alleyways. He never saw Private Connolly again.

Eventually cornered and captured Private Farr waited to be herded into a cattle truck destined for a prison camp. It was at this time Billy gratefully accepted a drink of water from a Dutch lady. Immediately, she was slashed across the face with the bayonet of one of the guards. Billy hit the guard before being clubbed unconscious.

Pte. William Farr

Arriving at the prison camp Billy was singled out and put into solitary confinement for six weeks. With almost no rations he only survived this ordeal by licking the damp moisture from the stone wall of his cell. Here, and for the remainder of his confinement, he would witness many atrocities committed by his captors.

Believed to have died in action, Billy's sister in Cwmbran received several distressing telegrams.

Liberated by the Americans, Billy, with other Eastern Valley veterans of Arnhem, returned home to a heroes welcome. At a reception in the Forge Hammer district of Cwmbran, the former prisoner-of-war was honoured and received gifts of appreciation from his friends.

A keen soccer player and winner of many darts competitions, Billy later worked as a welder at Girling Ltd, Cwmbran. When retirement arrived he received the firm's wristwatch for twenty five years service.

Following retirement Billy Farr developed a paraplegic condition which resulted in confinement to a wheelchair. This did not deter him from wanting to attend the 50th commemoration of the battle of Arnhem.

At Arnhem, in September 1994, Paratrooper William Farr saw his old comrades for the last time.

FRANCIS FRITH IN PONTYPOOL

he strange shaped van pulled by two well-kept horses trundled up the Eastern Valley road towards Pontypool. Its driver was already a dollar millionaire, and well on the way to making a second fortune.

At an early age Francis Frith went into business as a wholesale grocer in Liverpool and on reaching the age of 34 years, he sold up before becoming fully involved with the new and exciting subject of photography.

The year was 1868 and Frith had already received acclaim for a perilous photographic assignment in the Middle East. On his return to Britain he set himself the daunting task of compiling a photographic record of every city, town and village in the land. To enable him to do this his wife and children travelled with him and it was now the turn of Commercial Street, Pontypool, to be the subject of his cumbersome equipment.

Frith and Company rapidly became the largest photographic publishers in the world. Sadly, it was not until after Frith's death in 1898, that he became a household name. His two sons continued to run the business and in 1900 the Post Office brought in legislation that had a dramatic effect on the company's future development. For the first time postcards were permitted to be sent through the Royal Mail.

Frith had been a master craftsman and the magic of his large glass plate negatives would be seen in many shops throughout the country.

His descendants added to the already large collection of glass negatives over the years. Around 1970 the firm ceased to trade and the large premises in Reigate, which contained 60,000 old negatives, went up for sale.

A buyer could not be found for the collection and with the imminent demolition of the building, it appeared that the glass negatives would be in the path of a bulldozer.

Fortunately, a local historian, who was aware of the old negatives, contacted an internationally known firm who purchased the collection for promotional use.

The fate of the glass negatives was far from secure when the firm decided that they had no further use for the collection. As luck would have it an employee of the large firm bought the negatives with the aim of marketing what he named the Francis Frith Collection.

Recently the history of this unique and priceless collection of over 60,000 Victorian and Edwardian negatives reached its final chapter. The collection came into the safe keeping of the National Library of Wales and will be saved for posterity.

Perhaps a few inhabitants of the Eastern Valley still have a small piece of Frith history tucked away in their old photograph albums or in dusty attics.

Commercial Street, Pontypool.

THE QUIET DIGNITY OF VALLEY FOLK

t was a cold February morning in 1890 when William Williams carefully examined the pit shaft before stepping out of the cage-like structure to make his report. He was proud to be a descendent of Williams of Llanerch, who for many years had farmed the land on which could be found the colliery where he was employed. Within a short time of making his report an explosion occurred which claimed the lives of 176 men and boys of the Eastern Valley of Monmouthshire.

Everyone in Cook's Slope and nearby headings in the Llanerch Colliery had been killed. William Williams was one of the first to descend to see what damage had been done to the guides and framing of the pit; it would be an experience he never forgot.

In another part of the mine and seconds after the explosion, Michael Burchell, although badly shaken, gathered up two boys who had become unconscious from the effects of afterdamp. After wetting his scarf and placing it in their mouths he quickly carried them to the safety of the pit shaft.

Joe Phelps and his pal John Edwards were working in the Three Quarter Seam when the explosion occurred. Before cramming a scarf into his mouth to try to counteract the deadly after-damp, Joe called to his brother Tom, who worked nearby. Tom had survived and while holding on to each other, all three made their way to the pit shaft. On the way they had difficulty passing a horse which had been blown over and was lashing out in its death throes.

Stephen Bennett was lucky to escape death. The man who he was working with died immediately. Bennett fell unconscious on top of his body and there he remained until found by the colliery manager, who successfully revived him.

James Smith, Amos Sulway, Tom Rees, Ben Higgs, Walter James, and Phillip J. Powell (15), were among the survivors on that dreadful day in Eastern Valley history. Walter James suffered to the end of his days from the injuries and Phillip Powell would be the last survivor to pass away in 1966.

Mass graves were dug at different locations and the funeral cortege of one group burial stretched from Freehold Land, Pontnewynydd, to Trevethin Church.

With immense dignity the widows carried on with their lives and most never re-married. A fund immediately set up awarded each widow 5/- each week for herself and 2/6 for each child. Although helpful, and this amount would have paid the house rent in those days, the small amount of money proved inadequate and the widows, without grumbling, found employment.

Rhoda Walby (25), left with one son, resumed her profession as a nurse before qualifying as a midwife and practising in the district for forty years.

A Llanerch widow

Mrs Clara Thomas, of Zion Hill, Pontnewynydd, lost her husband (26), father and brother in the explosion. During her 58 years of widowhood she cherished a rose which her husband had given her. She dedicated her long life to the service of others and always read her bible at the beginning of each day.

Dinah Lewis lost her husband Lew and would be the last widow of the Llanerch disaster. Her only child, Priscilla, married John Davies of Ffrwd Road, and had four children. Dinah's granddaughter, Mrs Ethel Hughes, of Greenhill Road, Griffithstown, remembers when her grandmother would tell of how she kept the newspaper her husband was reading the night before the disaster, and of his favourite white scarf which she treasured for many years. Dinah Lewis passed away peacefully in 1957 on her 93rd birthday.

Little is left today to remind us of the tremendous loss felt by the families all those years ago, or their remarkable struggle for survival while remaining loyal to loved ones. A beautiful stained glass window, placed as a memorial, is tucked away in Trevethin Church and unseen by many folk. Due mostly to the caring actions of former Councillor George Day, a commemorative plaque will be found on the site of the Llanerch Colliery.

Prayer meeting at Llanerch colliery pit head

DOCTOR SLOPER'S DIARIES

ife in Pontypool during the first half of the 19th century was not only harsh, but brutal also. This is indicated in a collection of diaries in the possession of Professor John Sloper, of Rickmansworth, Kent.

These diaries give an exciting insight into Pontypool and district between 1824 and 1839.

Compiled by Professor Sloper's ancestor, one John Sloper, surgeon and apothecary, important entries shed light not only on the industrial and revolutionary times, but also the everyday happenings in the life of a busy local doctor.

John Sloper came to Pontypool around 1814 as an assistant to Dr. Phillips after signing an agreement that he would have to pay a £500 fine if setting up in practise on his own. He later married Mary Probyn, the daughter of a prominent Pontypool family in 1818. Following John Sloper's marriage, Dr. Phillips thought it was the right time to accept the young man as a partner and he began his practise in the Trosnant area of Pontypool.

Later he would move to the centre of Pontypool to live and practise medicine in Caroline Street, which now goes under the name of Commercial Street. In one of the houses in the row stretching from Pontypool Library to Barclays Bank, and on the river side of the street, Dr. Sloper earned a good living for those bleak days. This would also be supplemented by an apothecaries shop where potions were very much in demand, particularly on market days.

Dr. Sloper had four sons. Two went into medical practise, one became a wealthy tanner in Cardiff and gave rise to the naming of Sloper Road in the capital city, and the youngest, Henry, named after his uncle who was jailed for murder in Bristol, became a miner.

Dr Sloper's wife died following the birth of Henry in 1831. She had been of a fiery nature, and with another woman, was convicted of assault of a young boy in the town. A sentence of whipping was carried out in Usk Gaol.

Diary entries indicate that the small tract of land behind Caroline Street, between the house and river, would be used as private road for the delivery of horse-drawn goods to the apothecary shop. In addition to the entries of everyday living, mention is given to the two huge hammers in a nearby forge and his friendship with Chartist leader William Jones, watchmaker.

It appears that Dr Sloper enjoyed the oratories while attending Chartist meetings in Blackwood and William Jones would later lead the Eastern Valley insurrectionary band on the historic march towards Newport. Although most of them only reached the Greenhouse Public House in Llantarnam, he did not escape transportation to Van Diemen's land. Captain Muddle of the prison ship *Mandarin* gave the three Chartists leaders sympathetic consideration during the voyage by keeping them separate from the other prisoners. Having to wear convicts attire rankled the celebrity prisoners and although extremely fortunate to have a small cabin which had to accommodate the three of them, they still grumbled about their discomfort. Jones was also slow to mention in his letters that they had not been shackled for the voyage.

William Jones was soon to write to J. Sloper, Esqr, Surgeon & c, Pontypool, Monmouthshire, South Wales:

> "Mandarin at sea, off Cape of Good Hope,
> May 1st, 1840.

"Dear Sir, - Long before this you will have heard of the mitigation of our sentences However much it may accord with the wish of the public I assure you it is far from acceptable to me. Death with all its horrors is not half so bad as a life of slavery, misery and degradation.

"That our transportation is a source of gratification to the County Magistrates as men desirous of obtaining their elicit purposes to me is not surprising but that as Magistrates sworn to do justice and love mercy, they should exult in the punishment of the innocent is to me a matter of wonder.

"They well know that we are not guilty of that with which we were charged. The persons employed by them as spies knew well that our intentions were not treasonable and that the attack on the Westgate was never contemplated, and was only put in practice by the emissaries of the Magistrates, some of whom unfortunately fell as a sacrifice to their perfidy.

"We are now on our way to a strange land one in which the officers on board strive to persuade us we shall find a better chance of doing well than in that we have left. I hope if we remain this may be true but I am glad to say that they think also that there is every chance of our being pardoned.

"When you see Parker of Abersychan, give my respects to him as likewise all friends at Pontypool. I suppose Watkins and the rest of my late neighbours are as usual. I am in good health as I hope you are and all the family. Remember me to Charles and believe me.

> Yours Truly
> "Wm Jones.

"P.S. The Surgeon Dr A.M. Kechnie is particularly kind and allows us every indulgence his duty will allow him. The vessel is rolling from side to side desperately. We have had a very fine voyage so far. I hope it will continue and that I may have an equally fine passage to that home again from which after the decision of the judges I ought never to have been banished and for which Sir F. Pollack, Sir Wm Follett and Fitzroy Kelley, Esqr, there was nothing to justify the Government in doing.

> "W.J."

Dr. Sloper, Surgeon, died in 1848 and is buried at Trevethin Church where he had been a church warden for many years.

Professor Sloper's family still have the brass plate which advertised his ancestor's medical practise in Caroline Street all those years ago.

MR. WINTLE'S RAGGED SCHOOL

homas M. Wintle, the founder of the Pontymoile Undenominational Christian Mission, might well have said "I dwell among mine own people." He was born at Pontnewynydd, the son of a publican, on August 3rd, 1855. A limited education took place in the National School, Snatchwood, before he left at the age of fourteen years to start work in the British Ironworks.

By the age of seventeen years he showed such a capacity as a roll-turner that he became something of an expert in the iron trade and earned a man's wage. His leisure time was not so productive with intemperance, mischief and profanities deciding a sinful way of life.

At the age of twenty years this Godless life came to an end with the marriage to a good woman who was an active worker at St Peter's Church, Blaenavon. The sight of his young wife kneeling in prayer had a dramatic effect and he became converted before signing the pledge to abstain from alcohol.

His good work for over 30 years at Pontymoile began with the formation of a Good Templar's Lodge which saved hundreds from the drunkard's grave. He soon nervously gave his first Gospel address and it was while walking the canal side at Pontymoile that the ragged, unkempt, uneducated, half starved children of the district came to his attention.

At the back of his house in the Old Estate Yard, Pontymoile, a disused

Mr T.M. Wintle

granary was in no time turned into a Ragged School. The problem then arose how to gather in these savage children who were not very anxious to be 'improved.'

Armed with pockets full of sweets, Thomas Wintle and his helpers went in search of the little children who frequented the ironworks, canal bank, riverside and surrounding fields. Immediately they had a score of children - ragged, barefooted, and dirty, running around them and willing to go to school. The quality of life of

Ground Floor Plan

New Mission Hall and Institute, Pontypool, 1893.

W.Gilbertson & Kenrickner, Architects, London-Newport.

these children and many which followed were greatly improved.

Evangelistic services followed for everyone in the old granary with an iron hall erected nearby immediately overflowing with new members.

On March 2nd 1891, the large Mission Hall at Pontymoile opened, thus allowing Thomas Wintle to speak convincingly on human frailty, folly and sin.

This did not end the guerrilla warfare of open-air services and the Flat Stone of Cwmyniscoy still served a purpose. The stone lay by the roadside near a public house about half a mile from Pontymoile and Mr Wintle would regularly mount it as his pulpit. His outdoor fellowship increased in number, although sometimes there would be a threat to his physical self.

The Flat Stone of Cwmyniscoy

Throughout the years there would be many benefits from his work. During the 1893 recession, 100,000 meals were provided from the Mission Hall for the starving unemployed. Numerous young people did not feel the full force of the law due to his support and discharged prisoners from Usk Gaol were glad of his presence at the end of their sentence.

Colliery disasters were particularly traumatic for Mr Wintle's helpers. When visiting the homes of the bereaved and endeavouring to comfort them in their sorrow many painful and distressing scenes would be witnessed. Mr Wintle wrote of a colliery disaster victim who was a widower with eight children. The eldest girl, who had charge of the home, was only 17 years of age, and her grief was indescribable. As they sat by her side with her hand in theirs, she pitifully wailed:

'What shall I do without dad?' They pointed her to Jesus as the ever-present, never-failing friend, to which she replied: 'I know, sir, I know, but what shall I do without dad?'

With the long serving Mission Hall recently demolished to make way for a new road, the kind people of the nearby modern Mission Hall carry on the good work of Mr Wintle. The door of this friendly lighthouse in the Pontymoile district will always remain open to those who wish to hear the old, old story.

FOR ENGLAND, HOME AND BEAUTY

ith guns on fire they sailed into hell. Napoleon had for some time cast his eye longingly over the channel to Britain and it was only the Royal Navy at Trafalgar who would decide the fate of the small nation.

On board *HMS Victory*, Admiral Nelson gave orders to go through the enemy line. Before this could be achieved, the *Victory* had to receive heavy broadside fire from two enemy ships. The pell-mell battle of Trafalgar had begun in deadly earnest. Decks had been dowsed with sand to absorb the blood of battle, powder monkeys (small boys) ran to the ship's magazine to collect gunpowder, and the choking smoke and deafening noise of cannons firing, stretched the courage of the most disciplined sailor.

Cannons recoiled violently with each flash, before causing showers of deadly wooden splinters every bit as lethal as shrapnel or sniper fire from the enemies fighting tops. Some of the 800 crew felt the tearing of limbs and 30 men died before *HMS Victory* could begin to wreak havoc on the enemy.

Most of the British sailors present were at one time merchant seamen who had been the victims of heavily armed press gangs, intent on providing crews for the Royal Navy. Entered into military service under a false name and place of birth, they had no other option but to accept the hard life for a period of contracted time. Many would pass their days dreaming of what they would do with accumulated pay and prize money; the reward if an enemy ship was

HMS Victory

taken in battle. Many sailors favoured the purchase of a small beerhouse on their release from service.

The murderous firing on both sides continued. In the midst of the fighting Lord Nelson could be prominently seen on the quarter-deck in his full dress admirals uniform, complete with decorations. He was a conspicuous figure and a sharp-shooter's musket ball, from high up, ended his life.

Trevethin-born James Morgan would later tell of when he was aboard *HMS Victory* on the day Napoleon's dream of invading England ended for ever.

On November 6th, 1805, dispatches arrived in England giving news of the great victory and the lamentable death of Lord Nelson. This was followed by the news of the arrival of *HMS Victory* in Portsmouth.

For Rachy Shenkin Steven, a well proportioned popular lady who sold flannel in the streets of Pontypool on market day, the news would be the cause of great concern. Immediately she packed some belongings, before commencing the long mail-coach journey to Portsmouth to enquire about her son, James Morgan.

On arrival, reports indicated that Jim was unharmed and when reaching the quayside, she was placed precariously in a sling-chair and, to the cheers of the jacktars, hoisted up the towering side of the *Victory* to meet her son.

Arriving home in Pontypool, the Trafalgar veteran opened a beerhouse in High Street, to which he gave the appropriate sign, Nelson's Victory. There, for many years, he fought his battles over again, surrounded by tobacco smoke, and on planks more beery than bloody.

Married with six children he would later become a collier.

In June 1863, the man who had gone through the fiery hail at Trafalgar, and was known locally as 'Jem Victory,' died at Tranch Houses, Tranchwood, Pontypool, at 88 years. He was interred at the ancient Trevethin Church.

In 1885, an alehouse licence was issued to his son and the hostelry, later know as The Victory, situated between the Forge Hammer and Bridge End public houses, High Street, gave comfort to thirsty customers for well into the 20th Century. Demolition work eventually ended an interesting episode of Pontypool history.

THE LADIES of BLAENAVON

ost Eastern Valley industries owned small locomotives which gave valuable service for many years due to the expert care of engineering staff. As part of the industrial landscape, the warning of their approach could be heard by a shrill whistle, which mingled with other sounds of labour to form a now lost symphony of industry.

The successful Blaenavon Company Ltd was no different and profit made during the Great War allowed the replacement of some of their old second-hand locomotives. January 29th, 1915, saw the purchase of the locomotive named *Betty* for a fee of £1,350 and this was quickly followed by the acquisition of *Nan* at the higher cost of £1,840.

Built at the Caledonian engineering works of Andrew Barclay and Son, Kilmarnock, these small locomotives were brought by sea to Barry Docks before being transported by rail to Blaenavon.

Many of the old locomotives owned by the company only had numbers, but a new policy indicated that female names submitted by senior staff would adorn the sides of the new servants of the Blaenavon iron road. At the beginning of 1917, *Kibby* was bought for £930 and *Chrissie* for £2,130. It appears that a Scot, by the name of Mr Clements, was a senior manager at the

LYCEUM, NEWPORT.

"TOTO."

NEXT WEEK :
MONDAY TO FRIDAY AT 7.30. SATURDAY 7.15.

MARK BLOW
— PRESENTS —

"TOTO,"

by GLADYS UNGER,
Author of "Betty" and "Marriage Market."
the Famous Musical Comedy
from the Apollo Theatre,
London, with All-Star Cast,
— including —

LOUIS BRADFIELD
and DORIS LEE,

The Original "TOTO."

Box Office 10 to 1 and 2 to 6.
Phone 1905.

STUPENDOUS ATTRACTION.   Matinee Saturday at 2.30

"TOTO."

company and the saddle tank engines were immediately named after his daughters. The further purchase of *Lily* in September 1918 ended the female names in the Clements family and the naming of a further locomotive would be the cause of a mystery during more recent times.

Purchased on March 29th,1919 and costing £3,071, *Toto* would be the subject of a great deal of later speculation as to how the locomotive received its unusual name. Various suggestions were put forward. A clown thought to have visited Blaenavon with Sanger's Circus in 1919 became a possible answer to the mystery. This theory, although popular, lost out to a further suggestion that it was the name of a dog belonging to Mr Clement's daughter.

In-depth research has now revealed that the same week that *Toto* was bought, a famous musical comedy from the Duke of York and Apollo theatres, London, appeared at the Lyceum Theatre, Newport. The popular musical show, called Toto, was named after the main character of the story, a mischievous, good hearted Parisian hussy.

Many Blaenavon folk travelled to Newport to see the well-advertised show with an all-star cast. Oral evidence suggests that the actress, who played Toto (little flea), arrived in Blaenavon to promote the show by riding on the new locomotive, which bore a shiny brass plate with her stage name on it.

Another locomotive called *Nora* (£4,927) was bought in 1920 and also did service around the scattered Blaenavon Company undertakings. For many years these small locomotives pulled the colliers' train between Blaenavon and Garn-yr-erw and would be a welcome sight to the men when their shift ended.

With the decline of the Blaenavon Company, *Toto* was purchased by a syndicate of railway enthusiasts who completely restored the locomotive. Until recently she was exhibited and running at Mangapps Farm, Essex.

The Pontypool and Blaenavon Railway Society did excellent work restoring *Nora*, the only other existing Blaenavon Company locomotive. *Nora* has also been running well at the Society's site in Blaenavon, but requires attention to her boiler.

Perhaps one day *Toto* will return home to Blaenavon and, with *Nora*, again be a jewel in the Blaenavon crown.

THE SINGING OF BIRDS WAS NO MORE

amuel Mogford, a man of strong Baptist belief, brought his young family from Newport to Pontnewynydd as the result of a promise of better wages. While working as a roadman in a nearby colliery, further children were born at 5, Holyoake Terrace, and all attended the Merchants Hill Baptist Church.

As time passed, his children contributed to the family income by finding employment in the district. Ivor and Sam easily found work while their younger brother John took up employment at the nearby Llanerch Colliery.

A change of employment brought John even closer to home when he entered the Pontnewynydd Forge. It was here that the young lad enjoyed his work while standing alongside the sweat covered iron workers.

Life appeared complete for the sixteen year old with red hair, but events in a distant country would soon change his naivety.

He was on the afternoon shift when war with Germany commenced on August 4th, 1914. Early that historic morning he joined the throng of people in Commercial Street, Pontypool, to hear the latest news and views of those he thought wiser than himself.

Private John Mogford

Although underage, John Mogford was determined to play his part in the unfolding drama. On account of his youth, Mr and Mrs Mogford endeavoured to persuade him not to enlist. Mr Mogford even suggested that he would inform the authorities of his son's age, but John's mind was made up.

With other members of the Merchant Hill Baptist Church Sunday School, John received his Bible before going off to war with the 2nd Monmouthshire Regiment.

While witnessing the carnage any great war will produce, the young lad from Pontnewynydd soon matured.

On April 29th, 1915, he wrote home enclosing a card which indicated that he had distinguished himself with conspicuous bravery in the field while rescuing an officer from almost certain death.

In several of his letters he marvelled that after a cannonade had died down, the birds would again sing beautifully. Another letter, which would be his last, informed that he had finished with the famous 4th Division mining party and that he had become an orderly of Lieutenant W.J. Williams, of Pontypool.

On May 8th, 1915, the brave young man from Pontnewynydd died and he would have no known grave. His name will be seen on the Roll of Honour at the Menin Gate (panel 50), on the memorial gates at Pontypool, in the Regiment's history, and is included in the list of men and women who gave their lives from his local church

Of the few personal possessions returned to his parents, the blood stained Bible, previously presented by the Merchant Hill Baptist Church, became a poignant reminder of the youth who had given so much for his valley.

AN AFRICAN LOVE STORY

om Milsom began life in 1881 as one of five boys and four girls born to Mr and Mrs Frank Milsom, of Pentrepiod. He would have a remarkable life.

His first love was for horses and with unemployment present throughout the Eastern Valley, he joined the British Cavalry as a nineteen year old in August 1900.

During the latter part of the Boer War he was posted to the 7th Dragoon Guards in South Africa. Until the end of the war he served as an orderly to Captain E.P. Ford, of Pontypool.

The nature of the war in South Africa changed when the Boers became more successful by adopting guerrilla tactics, which involved fast raids on horseback. As quickly as they appeared, the horsemen escaped by using their knowledge of the vast countryside.

The British generals soon realised that the Boer commandos could only succeed if they continued to obtain food from the many homesteads found in the veldt.

A policy began of burning all farms and placing the women and children in a new form of confinement called concentration camps. Thousands of women and children died from disease and starvation in these camps.

Private Milsom was aware of

Tom Milson

this situation when he approached a small farm ahead of his mounted troop. Finding a mother with her teenage daughter, he quickly hid them in a nearby empty barn. The farmhouse and its contents became a mass of flames as the soldiers rode away. Milsom would later take many risks while delivering food and water to the frightened couple.

The Boer War came to an end. A further posting for two years in India did not prevent the Eastern Valley man from writing to the young girl he had met in the veldt.

Honourably discharged from the British Army, Thomas George Milsom immediately returned to South Africa to marry the teenage girl he had saved from possible death in a concentration camp.

Secure employment with the South African Mounted Police helped him to settle down to a new life with his wife Mellina.

Only on one occasion did he attempt to return to the Eastern Valley. His brother Joe was seriously ill and Tom booked his passage home. Sadly, Joe died before he left South Africa, and the trip was cancelled.

Tom retired from the mounted constabulary on pension in August, 1931. Following his retirement, Dingaan, the horse he had rode for 18 years while on duty, was presented to him at a special ceremony. (Dingaan was named after a bloodthirsty Zulu chief who succeeded the great Shaka). The famous charger was loved by the Milsom children for many years.

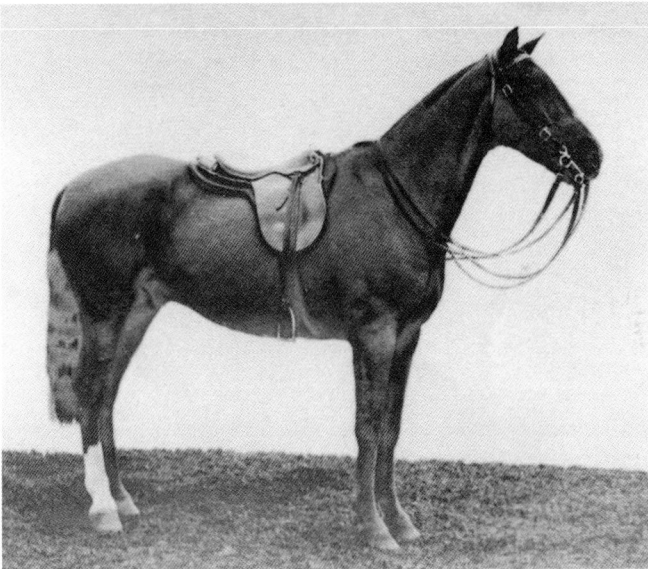

Dingaan

In 1947, the former Eastern Valley man and his wife were presented to King George VI and Queen Mary when the royal couple visited South Africa. At a garden party, he was introduced to the King as an old British soldier who married a Boer War refugee.

This brave and compassionate man died in 1951. He left a wife and grown-up family living in Wepener, Estcourt, Natal, South Africa.

TURN BACK THE CLOCK

I was young, of streamlined appearance, and could shift. The great Blaenavon athlete Ken Jones had been my role-model and along came a small collection of trophies.

The most memorable foot race which I took part was in 1960, and is always remembered by me as the Town Hall dash.

My work had taken me the short distance over the hills to Abergavenny and the warm weather was ideal for carnival week in the old market town.

For some unknown reason, my work colleagues urged me to take part in a road race in the centre of town. It had been said that around the year 1900, an athlete of some fame had performed a singular feat. At twelve mid-day, and on the first chime of the town hall clock, he set off down the road and reached the Swan Hotel before the twelfth chime sounded.

Upon examination of the course of the race, it was obvious that the former athlete must have had wings attached to his feet, yet the long-gone spirit of adventure still prevailed and I accepted the challenge.

My colleagues, while expertly assessing the form of each of the participants, were unusually attentive to my athletic needs leading up to Saturday.

Ten athletes stood at the starting line and were told that the race official would inform them when to get on their marks, followed by the command for the get-set position. The first chime of the town hall clock would signal the start of the race and the faint hope of achieving athletic immortality.

Over two thousand people lined the pavements on that humid August afternoon. The starting official, looking upwards, watched the movement of the minute hand on the large clock-face. Drawing on his long experience, he prepared us in the 'set' position.

Then it happened, or should I write, it didn't happen? For many years the town hall clock had faithfully served the inhabitants of the market town but on this occasion the large minute hand passed the 12 without ringing out its melodious chimes.

It transpired that the boys from the local rugby club had somehow gained access to the clock tower before temporarily sabotaging the chiming mechanism.

Around twenty minutes later someone arrived with a starting gun, and although the main reason for the race had been lost, we bolted down the long course.

With three-quarters of the distance covered, the race appeared mine. Then, without warning, and alongside W.H. Smith's bookshop, the excruciating pain in a calf muscle caused the race to be lost. My colleagues suggested that I had stopped at Smiths to purchase a book.

The incident of the town hall clock appeared in the national newspapers, and as I sit alone alongside my radiator, the memories of younger days come flooding back.